INVENTORS

PROFILES IN CANADIAN GENIUS

THOMAS CARPENTER

CAMDEN HOUSE

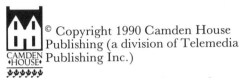 © Copyright 1990 Camden House Publishing (a division of Telemedia Publishing Inc.)

Canadian Cataloguing in Publication Data

Carpenter, Thomas, 1959-
    Inventors: profiles in Canadian genius

ISBN 0-920656-95-1 (bound) ISBN 0-920656-93-5 (pbk.)

1. Inventors – Canada – Biography –
Juvenile literature. 2. Inventions –
Canada – History –
Juvenile literature. I. Title.

T39.C37 1990   j609.22   C90-093908-7

Cover illustration by
Rocco Baviera

Trade distribution by
Firefly Books
250 Sparks Avenue
Willowdale, Ontario
Canada M2H 2S4

Printed and bound in Canada by
D.W. Friesen & Sons Ltd.
Altona, Manitoba, for
Camden House Publishing
(a division of Telemedia Publishing Inc.)
7 Queen Victoria Road
Camden East, Ontario K0K 1J0

Designed by
Linda J. Menyes

Colour separations by
Hadwen Graphics
Ottawa, Ontario

ACKNOWLEDGEMENTS

This book was written with the generous support of the Secretary of State whose Canadian Studies Directorate provided financial assistance and did so in a straightforward and encouraging manner.

I want to thank George Vosper, who gave liberally of his time and patiently explained the more complex details of Reginald Fessenden's accomplishments. I also wish to express my appreciation to researcher Christopher Baird and to Laurel Aziz for her assistance.

And finally, thank you to Camden House publisher Frank B. Edwards, who originally fostered the idea for this book and made its writing possible, and to staff members: editor Tracy C. Read; art director Linda Menyes; assistant editor Charlotte DuChene; copy editor Catherine DeLury; typesetter Patricia Denard-Hinch; editorial assistant Jane Good; publishing coordinator Mirielle Keeling; production manager Susan Dickinson; and associates Margo Stahl, Lois Casselman, Mary Patton, Christine Kulyk, Ellen Brooks Mortfield, Mary-Anne O'Connor, Peggy Denard and Johanna Troyer.

Although his father and grandfather had both been successful printers before him, Georges-Édouard Desbarats almost became a lawyer. When his mother died in 1839, Georges was only a year old. His father remarried, and the young boy, sent to study with the Jesuits, grew up in a series of boarding schools. Perhaps as a result, he showed little interest in joining the family business. At the age of 21, however, he finished his studies in law and left for Europe, where he reportedly visited the small city of Pau, in France, thought to be the traditional family seat and home of the family printing business.

Upon his return to Canada, young Desbarats began to feel the weight and attraction of that tradition. Over the next six years, he became increasingly involved in printing, and during the years before the senior Desbarats' death in 1865, Georges and his father together published 13 book titles. By the time he had inherited the family fortune and responsibilities, he was clearly committed to the publishing industry and enthusiastic about its future.

Unlike his father, Georges Pascal Desbarats, who prospered as a manufacturer and merchant and held the position of Queen's Printer, Georges-Édouard seemed drawn to the more flamboyant possibilities of the literary and editorial work associated with the printing profession. His father had managed his businesses with a canny skill that won him considerable wealth, but though Georges, too, was a businessman, he was not a terribly practical one. Indeed, his business failures eventually outstripped his triumphs. Yet in his own way, Georges-Édouard Desbarats the dreamer was a great success. He proved better at envisioning and founding magazines and newspapers than at making them profitable; but over the course of his career, he injected a great deal of life into the Canadian publishing industry.

From 1859 to 1864, Desbarats worked with his father in the official capacity of Queen's Printer, the printer of all government laws and documents. For an additional five years, he shared the position with a man named Malcolm Cameron. During that time, he also published a number of books, foremost among them the complete works of Samuel de Champlain in 20 volumes — over 9,450 pages. The printing plates for this monumental work were burned with his Ottawa factory in 1869, but a copy had been sent to the editor, Father Charles Honoré Laverdière, in Quebec City, and Desbarats simply started all over again. The maps and illustrations required to do justice to the grand scope of Champlain's life brought Desbarats his first experience with the printing of illustrations, and from that point on, the notion of illustrated journalism never left him. The power of pictures not only gripped his imagination but seemed certain to win that of his readers. Never doubting that illustration would become an integral part of the print medium, he clearly foresaw the course of journalism in the late-19th and 20th centuries.

During his tenure as Queen's Printer, Desbarats had published an official magazine called the *Canadian Gazette*, but the *Illustrated News* was his first venture into commercial publishing. It was by no means his last. One year after the *Illustrated News* was successfully launched, he brought out a French companion magazine called *L'Opinion Publique*, another illustrated work with 12 pages, four fewer than the *Illustrated News*. *L'Opinion* merged a year later with *L'Étendard National* of Worcester, Massachusetts, and the new paper, with a total circulation of 13,000, was sold two years later. In 1871, Desbarats bought *The Hearthstone* and promptly restyled it as a handsomely illustrated quarto, a publication which was printed on large sheets with the text arranged so that each paper could then be folded into four pages with printing on both sides. Stories and serialized novels by both Canadian and American authors were featured, and along with its new look, the small literary paper was also renamed. Under the title *The Favourite*, it was sold across the continent from an agency office in Boston.

Along with his more literary efforts, Desbarats also produced what the modern publishing industry calls trade magazines. In 1873, he brought out *The Canadian Patent Office Record, Mechanic's Magazine* and *The Canada Medical and Surgical Journal*. He did contract printing for governments, one year publishing 13,000 copies per month of *Le Journal d'Agriculture* for the Quebec government. In 1878, he started an eight-page weekly humour magazine called *The Jester*, which featured "bright and spicy" editorial content along with good cartoons. There were numerous other projects as well. Throughout his career, Desbarats worked at a breakneck pace, accumulating and spending vast amounts of capital and eventually losing the fortune left him by his father.

In 1887, having been buffeted throughout his career by the vicissitudes of the publishing industry, he scored an enduring triumph with *The Dominion Illustrated News*, a magazine he founded with the financial support of several renowned Canadians, including Sir Sandford Fleming. Although Desbarats died in 1893, the *Dominion Illustrated*, thanks to the photographic reproduction technology that Desbarats had helped pioneer, survived him by many years. Ironically, however, Desbarats' financial failures — *The Canadian Illustrated News* and *The New York Daily Graphic* — because they represented ground-breaking efforts in halftone photographic reproduction, were the sources of his greatest satisfaction. They also earned him a place in history.

Desbarats' active interest in the technology of his day especially suited him to the task of making halftone photographic reproductions a reality. It is rare for a new technology to be put into use so soon after its creation, but Georges-Édouard Desbarats and William Leggo worked well together. As an engraver, Leggo was familiar with the demands of the printing trade, and Desbarats' curiosity kept him closely involved with advances in printing techniques. These two men succeeded with commercial halftone printing almost a full decade before anyone else managed to achieve the same goal.

Some may think it odd that Georges-Édouard Desbarats is mentioned at all in the story of the first halftone and the birth of photographic journalism. Desbarats, after all, simply bought the technology that put the first halftone photograph in his *Canadian Illustrated News*; he was the first customer for a process actually created by William Leggo. But if Leggo brought to the endeavour the inventive genius, Desbarats had the foresight to invest in a new technology and the courage to risk his fortune bringing it into regular use. For understanding the importance of Leggo's work and for translating it into a commercial reality, Desbarats takes a place beside Leggo in the history of invention.

But what of William Leggo? His story is difficult to trace; it is even further obscured by his relationship with Georges Desbarats. He might have left clearer tracks had he not sold the company that bore his name to Desbarats in return for financial support and the opportunity to use his talents and new techniques on a widely circulated illustrated magazine. With his three brothers, Leggo had been working as an engraver in Quebec as early as 1860, but in all likelihood, he grew up and was trained in Europe. He and Desbarats met in the early 1860s, and to facilitate their increasingly close partnership, Leggo moved from Quebec to Montreal in July 1869. Only four months later, their combined energies brought forth the world's first published halftone, and together, they planned even greater things. When Desbarats took over the firm of Leggo and Company in January of the following year, it was a financial arrangement that gave Leggo the freedom to continue experiments with new equipment and to refine the existing techniques.

Beyond these details, information about William Leggo is scarce. But we know of the revolution in photojournalism he sparked, and we have a photograph from the pages of *The Canadian Illustrated News* showing a robust and jaunty-looking man with thick side-whiskers leaning on the box of a large camera.

It is not surprising that so few clues to Leggo's life remain. The fraternity of printers and engravers was a secretive and suspicious one. An individual's technique for transferring printed images onto paper was the basis of his livelihood and not something to be lightly shared. Chemistry was not well understood, and the intricate procedures required to produce printing plates were not unlike the veiled recipes of alchemists and witches. Patent protection and the expanding commercial printing industry were changing all that, but those who experimented with the puzzles of printmaking and photography were a close-mouthed group nonetheless.

Just as Georges Desbarats had come from a long line of printers, William Leggo's heritage was that of an artisan. Leggo and his brothers were all second-generation lithographers. Their father had been among the first students of the master Johann Aloys Senefelder in Munich, Germany, at the printing house Senefelder established only a year after discovering the basic methods of lithography in 1798.

Senefelder's process actually had precedents in the 16th century and was quite uncomplicated in practice. He simply discovered a new way to use the fact that water and oil or wax or grease will not stick together. However straightforward his techniques, they nevertheless formed the basis for a great deal of the more complex printing technology that has followed, including Leggo's innovations. The lithography — literally "stone writing" — learned by Leggo's father consisted of first drawing a picture onto a block of smooth, flat limestone using a greasy ink. The stone was then wetted, and the water was absorbed by the stone everywhere except where the lines were drawn. A second application of greasy ink spread across the stone with a roller would stick only to the dry areas where no water had soaked in. When a sheet of paper was pressed into place, the original image was reproduced. In an alternative method, chemicals that could not pass through the ink of the original drawing would be used to etch around the drawing, eating away a layer wherever the surface was unprotected. The drawing then stood out as a series of raised ridges that could be re-inked and used to press

WILLIAM AUGUSTUS LEGGO, 1871

a copy of the drawing onto a page. This raised-impression technique eventually became properly known as letterpress printing.

Although others had been experimenting with similar etching techniques for centuries, Senefelder's process provided the first dependable and commercially viable means of replacing the painstakingly hand-carved wood blocks that were locked into the printing press along with the lines of type.

For Leggo's father and his father's contemporaries, lithography introduced a startling new technology. Printers immediately recognized that it presented possibilities for mass-producing clear line drawings and printing out illustrations. Only 27 years after Senefelder founded his printing house, a man named Joseph Nicéphore Niepce produced the world's first photograph, opening another realm of illustration. For the printers and engravers of Leggo's generation, combining the speed of lithography with the accuracy of photography became the ultimate quest. Printers everywhere raced toward the same goal: a means of printing photographs. Two generations after Senefelder's work in Munich, William Leggo was grappling with the mysteries of photography in Quebec City and inching his way toward a practical solution to the problem of mass-printing copies of photographs.

Photographs were originally produced by coating either metal or glass plates with light-sensitive substances and then focusing the light that reflected from a scene or image through a lens onto the plate. As it reacted to the light, the sensitive material would rearrange itself into a copy of the image being viewed. The accuracy of the results astounded people. It was not at all clear, however, how this kind of image could be transferred onto even one sheet of paper. Photographs had too many shades of grey to be easily reproduced using existing printing methods. A printing plate made from a photograph produced merely a smudge when it was inked up and pressed against a sheet of paper. Early photographs came about as a result of experiments by engravers looking for better ways to produce the printing plates used to transfer ink onto a page. Printers were using light instead of etching chemicals or tools to carve pictures onto the printing plates, and some of the earliest "photos" were simply failed attempts to produce those plates. When Niepce discovered that the images of nature itself could also be captured on similar plates with the same perspective and detail as viewed with the human eye, a new art was created. Since photography was virtually born in the printer's shop, it was almost inevitable that a printer would discover a means of copying photographs into the papers and books that were mass-produced in those shops.

Photoengraving in all its forms was the process of producing printing plates using substances that were sensitive to light. Attempts to print illustrations from photographic originals were a natural outgrowth of the continuing evolution of plate-printing techniques. Printers like Leggo were already working toward a practical means of producing printing plates that involved making rudimentary photographs of simple drawings on the metal plate. The plate would then be treated so that ink would stick only where the light-imprinted image was formed. In this way, an inked reproduction of the original picture could be transferred onto a sheet of paper.

Photographs, however, still presented a difficult challenge to printers. Although a lithographic plate could place black ink on a white page, even photolithographic techniques could not cope with the countless shades of grey that also make up a photographic image. Some additional stage was required, and in this, halftone screens played an essential role. Originally, a halftone screen was simply a piece of glass with two sets of fine parallel lines scratched closely together on the surface in a grid. A piece of fine gauze cloth was used in early experiments, and even the scratched-line method used by Leggo made the picture look as though it had been printed on canvas. Conceived by Fox Talbot, the English pioneer of photography, as a means of producing a positive print from the negative in the camera, the screen was placed in front of the image as it was rephotographed in the preparation of the printing plates. The halftone screen cut up the continuous shades of a picture into a composite of thousands of tiny dots, and in this way, black ink and a white page could be used to produce all the subtle shades of grey.

Without any dots at all, the blank page is white. But halftones work on the principle that as you move tiny black dots onto a piece of white paper, the paper appears to change colour. The eye sees ever darker shades of grey as the size of the dots increases, until finally, the page is filled in as solid black. In a printed photograph, the different shades in the picture are represented by areas where there are larger or smaller dots.

A good deal of experimentation was necessary to achieve an effective screen for creating halftones, and although American pioneers Frederic E. Ives and the Levy brothers, Louis and Max, standardized the manufacture of screens in the 1880s, it was one of the problems that Leggo had to overcome 20 years earlier. Halftone screens alone, however, did not allow for the mass production of photographs, and Leggo's true triumph was in discovering a practical means of photoengraving. He called it Leggotype, and with his engraving method, he could quickly and with relative ease copy any picture onto a printing plate and run off copies. Illustrations could be prepared for publications without hand-drawing them onto lithographic stones or carving them into printers' woodcuts. Illustrations could even be copied from other magazines and papers at a fraction of the cost of the originals; using a halftone screen, photographs from cameras could be transferred to a printing plate and onto the page. Compared with the painstaking and time-consuming task of creating a drawing or a woodcut, using photographs must at first have seemed like cheating.

As a skilled printer, Leggo had other techniques at his disposal, including engraving, lithographing, type printing and his own patented method of electrotyping — another specialized means of preparing printing plates. His unique specialty, however, remained the photolithographic Leggotype.

Desbarats and Leggo patented the process, then advertised it to win backing for their publishing plans. In May 1866, *The Philadelphia Photographer* reported:

"We have received from the inventors, Messrs. G.E. Desbarats and W.A. Leggo, of Quebec, C.E. [Canada East], some specimens of what they term 'Leggotypes,' or 'Photo-electrotypes' — done upon a common hand printing press — by their patented process. The object of the patentees is to produce electrotype plates of pictures, ready for common printing, like ordinary type printing, without engraving or other hand work. The process is briefly as follows: upon the varnished side of an ordinary negative, pour a solution of gelatine containing bichromate of potash. Dry, and expose the uncoated surface uppermost to light, which fixes that portion of the bichromate upon which the rays fall. Dissolve off the unfixed portion by dipping in warm water; drain, and we have a film upon the glass more or less raised, according to the strength of the lights in the picture. Take an impression of this film in plaster. Dip the impressed plaster in hot wax, and place the waxed surface upon a glass plate also covered with hot wax. The wax upon the plate unites with the wax upon the plaster, and the latter may then be removed, leaving upon the plate a facsimile in wax of the original photographic

DETAIL SHOWS ENLARGEMENT OF HALFTONE

gelatine film. The facsimile being now dusted with plumbago and elec-
trotyped in the usual manner, a printing block in copper is produced,
capable of use with printer's ink upon any press."

In simpler terms, Leggo's process involved coating a negative (just
like the negatives for modern black-and-white photographs) with a sub-
stance that hardened when exposed to light. When a light was shone
through the negative image, it was partially blocked out, but where it
penetrated, it solidified those areas which were to show up dark in the
final picture. So when the remaining unhardened "gelatine containing bichromate of potash" was washed away, a raised positive image
was left behind like a rubber stamp, and the image was then transferred
to the printer's plate. Ink was applied, and the image was pressed onto
a blank sheet of paper to produce the final picture. Even a brief expla-
nation suggests the complexity of printing techniques in the mid-19th
century. Leggo's mastery of new techniques earned him the financial
backing he needed to implement them; in turn, his mastery supported
Georges-Édouard Desbarats' faith in illustrated journalism. His inven-

tive skills played a crucial role in the fundamental shift toward the assumption, unique to the 20th century, that the exchange of information and telling of news should be accompanied by a visual image.

The Canadian Illustrated News survived for 14 years, genteelly presenting book reviews, gossip and Victorian novels in serial form. Short on social comment, it did not grapple with contentious political issues. Yet most 19th-century periodicals were fiercely partisan and were used to spread the personal opinions of the people who owned them. *The Canadian Illustrated News* distinguished itself by the even-handed and objective style it brought to the issues it reported. For historians in the century since it was published, it has also proved to be a valuable repository of photographs that were unavailable from any other source.

On December 28, 1883, the *Illustrated News* folded, according to the then publishers, "for the simple reason that its issue is not remunerative to the Company who publish it." Desbarats himself had sold the magazine in 1874 when its circulation stood at 7,000, and he withdrew entirely from the endeavour in 1879 after a 10-year involvement, a decade in which he had also busied himself with many other projects. For a number of years, the magazine's unique format kept it afloat in a very competitive and unpredictable industry, despite the fact that Canada's small population made the survival of a national publication unlikely. The true measure of Leggo and Desbarats' accomplishment, however, was their launching of *The New York Daily Graphic* in 1873, the first illustrated daily in the world. Huge amounts of capital were attracted to this project, and the confidence of the important investors rested on Desbarats and Leggo's demonstrated success printing both hand-drawn and photographic illustrations.

The remarkable achievements of *The Canadian Illustrated News* have often been overlooked by historians of photography. Credit for the first published halftone is often given to a man named Stephen H. Horgan, who printed the first newspaper photograph in *The New York Daily Graphic* in 1880. The revolution that actually began in 1869 with the first issue of *The Canadian Illustrated News* is often mistakenly ascribed to the famous American paper. In any case, there has been no historical injustice. The men who brought about the advances made at the *Illustrated News* were the very people who went on to establish the New York paper. Horgan's historic photograph was printed with a method he learned from William Leggo, using one of Leggo's half-

Carbide Willson's career ended abruptly, but his influence persisted. A quiet man with an almost intuitive understanding of the potential of electricity and chemicals, Willson conceived plans on an immense scale and undoubtedly had a profound effect on the patterns of Canadian industrial development in the 20th century. But even he did not foresee the significance of his greatest accomplishment. Henry Ford's introduction of assembly-line manufacture is often identified as the second great wave of industrial expansion, but it was acetylene, with its ability to cut steel into any shape, that moved industry out of the age of the blacksmith and into the modern era. As a businessman and even more as an innovator, Willson would have been pleased both that his navigational buoys were replaced by something better and that brighter, cheaper, more convenient electric lights won out over acetylene lamps. He loved change and improvement, and it is impossible to guess what further contributions he might have made had he lived on into the years of spectacular technological progress between the two European wars. Had he survived, he would have seen acetylene shaped into a host of new products, from industrial solvents to synthetic rubber and plastics. The self-taught inventor who had begun his career with a single quavering light shining from the window of a Hamilton smithy would no doubt have approved.

REGINALD FESSENDEN

ON THE AIR

In the last years of the 19th century, electricity lit up the night with a cleaner, brighter light than had ever been seen before. It powered streetcars and began to drive the wheels of industry at greater and greater speeds. Unfortunately, hot wires, poorly insulated and plastered into the walls of people's homes, acquired a deserved reputation for starting fires that threatened to kill the young electricity industry. At his laboratories, Thomas Edison responded to the menace by handing the problem over to an untrained, inexperienced 21-year-old Canadian named Reginald Aubrey Fessenden, who found an answer and, in the process, rewrote humankind's fundamental understanding of the structure of atoms, the building blocks of the material world.

The son of a poor Anglican minister, Reginald Aubrey Fessenden came by his intellectual powers naturally. His mother was the journalist and well-known nationalist Clementina Fessenden, and her father was Edward Trenholme, inventor of the grain elevator, the grain cooler and the railroad snowplough. The Trenholmes were a family of strong-willed, independent-minded people, and the house that Clementina and her siblings kept in Montreal while they attended school was a meeting place for young people drawn to the Trenholmes' modern ways and outspoken opinions. One of those young people was Elisha Fessenden, and on January 4, 1865, he and Clementina were married. In the fall of the following year, their son Reginald was born.

Reginald's earliest remarkable skill was language. The boy who had read Edward Gibbon's *The History of the Decline and Fall of the Roman Empire* at age 7 was teaching Greek and French at Bishop's College School in Lennoxville, Quebec, by the time he was 16. Along the way, he had won a scholarship to De Veaux Military College in Niagara Falls, New York, and attended Trinity College School in Port Hope, Ontario. At Bishop's, Fessenden taught classes during the day and went to classes in the evenings to "gain some insight into higher mathematics," as he put it in a letter home.

Fessenden made it a lifelong habit to gain insights and to confront difficult problems by returning to first principles and grounding himself in the most essential and fundamental knowledge he could acquire. Although he left Bishop's to accept a teaching position at the Whitney Institute in Bermuda, those first studies in mathematics marked the beginning of his extraordinary career. An uncle, Cortez Fessenden, also played a crucial role in his early development. An educator and co-author of the first Canadian physics textbook as well as an amateur inventor, Cortez taught his nephew an abiding respect for pure science and mathematics while also imbuing him with a deep enthusiasm for the glories of technological progress. Throughout his career, Fessenden would approach each new problem by rejecting accepted theories and rebuilding from the ground up.

Compared with the frenetic activity of the following years, Fessenden's stay in Bermuda was a quiet time, a time for self-examination and for gathering strength. On his first day there, he met Helen Trott, a fellow teacher whose family had settled on the island. Working together and later sharing the island's limited social life — which was often centred around the Trott family dinner table — the two young people became friends as well as intellectual allies. Helen must have glimpsed something trustworthy in the eccentric and intense young man. They became engaged, even as Fessenden made plans to leave the island. A remarkable woman herself, Helen had likely drawn her own conclusions about Reginald Fessenden and his schemes. Yet even she must have experienced some doubt when Fessenden announced that he would go to New York and acquire the learning and experience he needed to become — as he had already predicted he would — the inventor of wireless telephones. Dissatisfied with teaching and charged with equal measures of scientific enthusiasm and self-confidence, Fessenden sailed from Bermuda to New York City in 1886. After taking a room in a boardinghouse, he presented himself at Thomas Edison's Llewellyn Park laboratory

Fessenden was not the first to make that particular pilgrimage. Many ambitious young scientists had flocked to the inventor whose creations were changing the face of society and whose fame had already made him a legendary hero of American culture. In response to the calling card sent in by Fessenden, Edison fired back a note asking a single question: "Do you know anything about electricity?" With uncharacteristic modesty, Fessenden, who already possessed an impressive grasp of mathematics as well as a self-taught understanding of the theories behind electricity, answered, "No, but I learn quickly." Edison terminated the correspondence by declaring, "I already have enough men who know nothing about electricity." A full year passed before Fessenden found himself back at the Edison laboratories.

During those first months in New York, Fessenden took on writing assignments for the *New York Herald Tribune*, turning out articles that earned him $5 apiece. To gain the practical experience with electricity that he lacked, he passed his time at construction sites pestering the foremen until he finally landed a job testing the wires that Edison's own company installed in the streets of Manhattan. He proved so adept at handling the machinery and taking careful readings with the "galvanometer" that, within months, a series of promotions placed him back where he wanted to be, at Edison's side doing laboratory research and helping to shape the ideas of the future into practical reality.

The quality of Fessenden's mind and the freshness that his self-education brought to existing problems impressed Edison immensely. He encouraged the young man's propensity for avoiding the pitfalls and prejudices of accepted theories, and together, they worked on constructing improved dynamos. Reminded of their first exchange of notes, Edison conceded regretfully that he must indeed have been in a foul mood that day. Already he knew that Fessenden's ignorance could be more valuable than the lifelong experience of other men.

When Edison faced the critical need for flameproof wire insulation, he charged Fessenden with the task of finding a material that could not only resist oil, water and acids but could also be folded and twisted like rubber without cracking during installation. It would be decades before plastics provided a solution to the problem facing Fessenden, and although there were many materials at that time which resisted corrosion, very few offered the necessary elasticity.

The assignment was deceptively simple. Instead of experimenting with various compounds, Fessenden set about tracking down the root of the problem, eventually conducting studies of even the most basic structures of matter. As Edison had undoubtedly expected he would, Fessenden immersed himself in the theories of physics and chemistry and, ignoring the conventional wisdom of his day, tried to find out for himself why certain materials were elastic and why they caught fire when heated. Eventually, he concluded that excess hydrogen atoms made rubberlike substances flammable and that hydrogen could be replaced by chlorine atoms without making the resulting material too brittle. Subsequent experiments proved him right. The pungent chlorine soaked his skin, hair and clothes and imparted a strangely unromantic scent to the letters he wrote to his fiancée in Bermuda; but in the end, he delivered the necessary insulating compound, thereby guiding the electricity industry past a major roadblock.

Fessenden's research into the nature of matter led him to two conclusions: that the components of atoms possessed matching positive and negative charges which held them together; and that the quality of elasticity in rubber was determined by the nature of those electrical relations. Such insights brought him into direct conflict with perhaps the most famous and respected scientist of his day, Lord Kelvin, the great University of Glasgow physicist. "Obviously," argued Lord Kelvin, "the fact that rubber particles stick together cannot possibly be due to electricity. Every physicist knows that it is because of gravitation." A few years later, Fessenden claimed that "an inventor must never be intimidated by what appear to be facts when he

REGINALD AUBREY FESSENDEN

knows they are not." His laboratory work contradicted Kelvin's position, and his published articles subsequently proved the point. Twenty years later, physicists following the lead of giants like Niels Bohr and Ernest Rutherford would begin to talk about atoms in terms similar to those used by 25-year-old Reginald Fessenden, who discerned the basic structure of the atom on the way to creating a better fireproof rubber insulation for electrical wires.

Part of Thomas Edison's ambition as a young man was to use the fortune he had earned from his early telegraph inventions to establish a facility that would provide "inventions-for-hire" as well as pursue new projects. Not long after Fessenden's first success, Mr. Pratt of the Pratt & Lambert Paint Company Ltd. paid a visit to the Edison laboratories. Mr. Pratt was looking for ways to improve the quality of his varnishes. Edison sent him to see young Fessenden, by now the head of the chemistry division. Fessenden had experimented with hundreds of substances in his work on insulation and almost immediately suggested mixing Zanzibar gums into varnish, an innovation that produced a beautiful shiny finish that was both cheaper and longer-lasting.

Pratt and Lambert were so impressed that they offered the self-taught chemist a full partnership in their company with an extravagant annual salary, doing their best to lure Fessenden away from the Edison fold. Fessenden, however, had other plans. The seeds of many of his greatest inventions had already been planted. Edison's facilities, with their powerful emphasis on transforming raw science into technology, suited him perfectly. In the extensive library and laboratories, Fessenden was educating himself, preparing to pursue his greatest dreams. He turned Pratt and Lambert down, just as he would refuse other tempting offers in the future. In the often-impoverished years that followed, he never gave any sign that he regretted his decision.

Fessenden's three-year tenure with Edison undeniably made him a chemist, but his success with wire insulation was followed by experiments with electricity as well. He tailored the special dynamo that Edison required for his moving-picture equipment and ransacked the vast Edison technical library for information about wireless voice transmission, combing through dozens of journals and contemporary reports. In 1887, when Germany's Heinrich Hertz, the discoverer of electromagnetic radiation, succeeded in causing a spark on one side of his laboratory to ring a bell on the other side of the room, he also caused a great leap of excitement in Reginald Fessenden on the other side of the ocean. With his co-worker Arthur Kennelly — the man who would one day discover and explain the nature of the earth's ionosphere — Fessenden waited impatiently for the first written reports about "Hertzian Waves." In time, Hertzian theory occupied his every waking hour.

In the late 1880s, the Edison companies suffered a series of setbacks, and Fessenden and his colleagues found themselves unemployed. Refusing to let this interfere with his plans, he married Helen Trott in September 1890 in New York City. Years later, one of Helen Fessenden's favourite stories was of Reginald sitting beside her in Central Park after the wedding ceremony confessing that he had spent all of his money on a 22-karat-gold wedding ring and a diamond brooch from Tiffany's. He had not considered the problems of food and a room, and the couple had to use Helen's money to purchase their train tickets to Chippewa, Ontario, where they spent their brief honeymoon visiting with the Fessenden family.

Fessenden's work now began in earnest. His time with Edison had exposed him to the leading edge of both science and practical innovation and had transformed a talented young dreamer into a strictly disciplined researcher and inventor. He found a position in Newark, New Jersey, with the United States Company, a subsidiary of the famous company founded by George Westinghouse, inventor of the air brake for trains. After being laid off once again in 1892, he accepted an academic post at Purdue University, in Lafayette, Indiana.

During his brief time with Westinghouse, however, Fessenden had made yet another discovery that profoundly affected the young electricity industry. In the 20th century, the light bulb has become synonymous with brilliant ideas. It had indeed been the perfect invention, a stroke of Thomas Edison's genius. But Edison held the patent on the light bulb, giving him exclusive control of a market that George Westinghouse wanted to pursue. Only a few years after the light bulb's discovery, Reginald Fessenden was handed the task of reinventing the little gadget. And that was exactly what he proceeded to do.

The original light bulb relied on fragile platinum wires to pass electricity through the glass of the bulb. The material was expensive and the technique was patented, so lighting remained costly and limited in its uses. But in short order, Fessenden circumvented the existing patents and made a significant improvement in design. In place of platinum, he discovered an iron alloy and a nickel alloy that could be fused to the glass of the bulb and used to supply electricity to the filament inside the vacuum of the bulb itself. The design won new patents and earned Westinghouse the contract for the 1893 exposition at Chicago. Tens of thousands of people saw the miraculous new lights, and a vast popular market was born. The cheaper, longer-lasting bulbs revolutionized the industry.

During the same period, Fessenden came up with the solution to a problem plaguing the designers of electric motors and transformers: electric motors were overheating, and there appeared to be no remedy. With his unique understanding of the nature of atoms, Fessenden concluded that the cause of excess heat was the behaviour of carbon atoms in the steel used to build the motors. This in itself was a considerable discovery. He then set about designing a new kind of steel, determining that carbon atoms in the steel could be replaced with silicon atoms to produce an alloy which would not overheat. His solution has never been bettered, and silicon steel has remained to this day the standard material for the construction of all electrical motors.

Once at Purdue, Fessenden found himself with the time and the facilities to pursue his own interests. His infectious passion for research and for the potential of new technologies, along with his education in the classics and his considerable skill as a linguist, made him a very popular lecturer. Fessenden's new position was short-lived, though, as less than a year after he began, George Westinghouse endowed a new chair of electrical engineering at the University of Pittsburgh and recommended that his former employee be offered the position. In September 1893, Fessenden took up his new post and entered what has been described as the most productive and creative period of his life, a time during which he became obsessed with the notion of radio telephony — voices transmitted without wires.

Yet while the famous Guglielmo Marconi began to fire his wireless messages over the Salisbury Plain and across the English Channel, Fessenden struggled merely to transmit across his laboratory. He tinkered endlessly with his equipment, always improving it, but was never quite satisfied. The instrument that caused him the most grief played a crucial role in receiving signals and could not be dispensed with. Called a coherer, the small tube contained tiny iron filings that reacted to each individual incoming signal by lining up in a fashion similar to filings exposed to a magnet, forming a bridge which allowed the small spark to pass. Just barely adequate for transmitting Morse code, it seemed almost useless for Fessenden's purposes. It could not react nearly fast enough to capture the subtle complexity of voice messages.

Even as he worked at replacing the coherer with something better, however, Fessenden realized that he had to grapple with a much more fundamental problem. He still did not have an adequate grasp of the theory behind wireless transmission. Although he knew that signals could be beamed from a transmitter and that they would cause some reaction in a receiver, neither he nor anybody else in the world clearly understood what happened in between.

Fessenden's conclusion about the true nature of radio transmission came during a train ride. After exhausting months of research, he finally fit the pieces together as he rode from Toronto to Peterborough, Ontario, where he was enjoying a much-needed vacation. Wireless signals, he decided, did not need to be mere blasts of energy rocketing straight from the transmitter to be caught by a receiver. Treated properly, they would form a continuous wave emanating from the source and spreading out through the air like ripples from a pebble dropped into the water. Morse code could already be sent by starting and stopping the waves — long blasts for dashes and shorter ones for dots. But far more important, Fessenden determined that voice or even music could be carved onto a continuous stream of waves and carried across the open air to a receiver.

TWIN RADIO TOWERS, COBB ISLAND EXPERIMENTAL SITE

His continuous-wave theory provided the insight that set Fessenden apart from others who struggled with the secrets of wireless transmission. For one thing, he now knew exactly why the coherer could not work. And he also knew precisely what he had to do: design a machine capable of producing an endless signal of radio waves, carriers for his voice messages.

As Fessenden envisioned, radio waves work like an invisible conveyor belt. The message placed at one end travels along until it is scooped up by a receiver. The belt continues to move even when nothing is being carried. If no message is transmitted, then only silent radio waves travel through the air. Fessenden demonstrated that the sound waves of voices or music could be made to change the shape of the radio waves like a message scratched onto the surface of the conveyor belt and thus could be carried over great distances. At the source, he "added" sound waves to the radio waves, and at the receiving end, he "subtracted" the radio waves, leaving the sound message intact.

Fessenden returned to Pittsburgh in late August 1896 charged with

THE BASE OF THE TOWER, BRANT ROCK, MASSACHUSETTS

renewed passion and confidence. He plunged back into his research, quickly bending old ideas and technical theories to fit his new understanding. The experiments brought a string of successes, and by November, Fessenden and his assistant Mr. Kintner had begun to cover fresh ground. In a few months, he progressed further than he had in all the years before, redesigning much of the machinery he needed in the process. Yet even the research time available to him as a professor was not enough for his purposes. As word of his experiments spread, he began looking for a better position.

By March 1900, Reginald, Helen and their 8-year-old son Reginald Kennelly, along with their cat and a new research assistant, were installed at Cobb Island, in the Potomac River . In a demonstration for the U.S. Weather Bureau, Fessenden had so impressed his audience with the ease with which his wireless system could transmit and receive Morse code that he was hired at an annual salary of $3,000. Settled into crude accommodations on the island, he set up his equipment and soon had his invisible messages winging out over the land and the sea.

FESSENDEN, SEATED, AND THE BRANT ROCK STAFF, JANUARY 30, 1906

Fessenden startled even his employers with the clarity of the Morse code messages he transmitted back to the receiving tower that had been erected at Capitol Hill in Washington. The first year-long contract proved such a success that the operation expanded, and the Weather Bureau sent Fessenden on to Roanoke Island, off the coast of North Carolina. As the number of stations increased, he continued his own research into wireless telephony.

Eventually, Fessenden secured private financial backing from a pair of Pittsburgh millionaires named Thomas H. Given and Hay Walker Jr. Together, they formed the National Electric Signaling Company and set up a research station at Brant Rock, on the coast near Boston, Massachusetts. But the story of Fessenden's work on the coast — on Cobb and Roanoke islands and finally at Brant Rock — is not only a tale of scientific research and glorious success but also a pitiful list of broken contracts, manipulation and dishonesty. Only Fessenden's great physical strength and endurance saw him through the former; only his strength of character sustained him through the latter.

Both the Weather Bureau and his later partners ignored Fessenden's vision of transmitting voice without wires: each considered telegraphy the only important goal. Radio was an impossible dream, they said, at best a useless toy. Nonetheless, Fessenden carried on his work in secret. He had no trouble keeping his backers satisfied, because with each improvement to his voice equipment, his telegraph system also benefited. Sending dots and dashes, in fact, was becoming child's play for the machinery he had dubbed the "Fessenden System."

Just nine months after arriving at Cobb Island, Fessenden orchestrated the world's first voice transmission. Two moves and two years later, on January 3, 1906, he made the first successful two-way transatlantic telegraph transmission only days after the erection of his towers. He was also the first to send voice across the ocean and the first to make a long-distance transmission over land, from Brant Rock to New Orleans, in 1906. And on Christmas Eve of the same year, he made the first broadcast from a single transmitter to several receivers at once. Like the broadcasts of the radio stations that would one day blanket the continent, his Christmas Eve programme included both music and conversation. His unlikely audience consisted of sailors on United Fruit Company cargo ships, which carried equipment for receiving Morse code messages listing the changing big-city prices for their products. The sailors steaming north from the tropics must have suspected a divine Christmas miracle when their telegraph machines suddenly broke into speech and then sang them a song. The voice they heard, however, was that of Reginald Fessenden himself, beaming out from his radio towers at Brant Rock, first reading from the Bible and then playing the violin as he sang *O Holy Night*. Edison's phonograph — itself still a rather novel item — was also used to play Handel's *Largo*.

It was during frenzied preparations for the historic broadcast that another of Fessenden's minor inventions came in handy. Throughout his career, Fessenden's active imagination threw off ideas like spinning fireworks. To control the clutter on his desk, he had invented microphotography, and to summon his staff from the various buildings at the Brant Rock site, he invented a version of the pocket pager, which users placed in their headgear. One day, hats started buzzing all over the station. Workers rushed to the 400-foot main transmitting tower, where they discovered their distinguished employer stuck fast in a cylinder surrounding the ladder to the top of the mast. Comfortable living had given Fessenden a girth to match his impressive stature. Un-

OPERATORS AT THEIR POSITIONS, BRANT ROCK

fortunately, he had become just an inch too large around the middle and was now wedged tightly into the ladder passage. On the brink of making history, the world's greatest radio pioneer had to be stripped naked and rubbed with grease so that he could slip back down to the ground. Instead of shedding weight, however, Fessenden chose to rig up a bosun's chair on the outside of the tower, and he completed his preparations swinging in midair, 400 feet above the ground.

The first transatlantic voice transmission, a far greater accomplishment than a mere broadcast, had, in fact, occurred accidentally a month before the eventful Christmas. Fessenden himself learned of it when he received a registered letter from his assistant Mr. Armor at the Machrihanish station in Scotland: "At about 4 o'clock in the morning, I was listening in for the telegraph signals from Brant Rock when, to my astonishment, I heard, instead of dots and dashes, the voice of Mr. Stein telling the operators at Plymouth how to run the dynamo. At first, I thought I must be losing my senses, but I am sure it was Stein's voice, for it came in as clearly as if he were in the next room." Weeks and

BOMBARDIER WORLD WAR II ARMOURED TROOP TRANSPORT

Bombardier's track system and construction techniques could be modified to create an all-terrain vehicle. In the snowy northern battlefields of Europe, the brainchild of the inventor from tiny Valcourt would give Allied troops an important newfound speed and manoeuvrability. The Canadian government asked him to design a winter troop carrier, and Bombardier promptly modified his B12 model, adding artillery mounts and oversized tracks as well as extra doors and a hatch on the roof. It won immediate approval. In conjunction with army engineers, he proceeded to develop several new machines. And although commercial sales of his own products were restricted by the wartime government, the Bombardier operation continued to expand: 150 troop carriers with added armour were built in Montreal and sent overseas. They were followed by one of Bombardier's most revolutionary vehicles, the legendary Penguin, a sleek, low-profile body slung over wide tracks that extended the full length of the machine and flared up at the front, ready to surmount any obstacle. Designed to confront far more than just snow, it was unstoppable, adaptable to virtually any conditions and terrain. Compared with the comfortable, rounded form of his buses and snow cars, the Penguin did indeed look like a stark military machine, and from the snows of northern Europe, the influence of Bom-

PROUD INVENTOR OF THE MUSKEG TRACTOR

bardier's machines now reached as far south as the Mediterranean and even into the South Pacific.

The war could have spelled disaster for someone in Bombardier's position. His inventions were protected by patents, but the war years swallowed up much of the precious time available before emerging competitors would legally be able to copy his ideas. Contracts with the government, however, had also strengthened the company and enabled it to expand its operations, and now Bombardier the ingenious inventor also had to become a canny businessman and marketing strategist. Sales boomed in the years immediately following the war, but as roads and automobiles improved, the demand for his large snow machines inevitably declined. The answer, Bombardier recognized, was careful diversification—new machines designed to solve other kinds of problems.

Bombardier's snow machine, shaped like a giant jellybean with thundering tracks and tiny skis sticking out in front, was now adapted and sometimes completely redesigned for use in a bewildering variety of exotic locales. Bombardier filled contracts for the French Foreign Legion and gave them vehicles for use in the Sahara Desert. After studying the problems of the logging industry, he designed machines capable of powering themselves into the bush and being loaded with large piles of logs. Orders came from Peruvian sugarcane plantations, where mud, not snow, made travel impossible by ordinary means. Bombardier machines were used to lay oil pipe in Scotland. And Bombardier designed one of his most famous vehicles for use by oil-exploration crews in western Canada. The Muskeg Tractor, named for the deep northern bogs of ancient leaves and moss, could be driven over swampy areas where even a person walking might sink waist-deep into the muck. Sir Vivian Fuchs, the Antarctic explorer, returned the Muskeg Snowmobile to its native element in 1957 and travelled over Antarctic snows to the South Pole with a speed and comfort that had never before been imagined. He described his Bombardier machine as "outstandingly rugged, even at 60 below," and added, "We all have great affection for the Muskeg."

All of his adult life, Armand Bombardier had laboured earnestly to design practical, useful vehicles: machines that conquered the winter snows, delivering mail or schoolchildren or emergency service; machines to carry lumberjacks deep into the bush and to push oil exploration into the northern wastes. Yet because of his last great invention, the Ski-Doo, Bombardier's name, for most people, conjures up images of winter fun.

The inventor's name might well have disappeared along with his large round-backed Quebec snow cars, remembered only in frontier regions as a line of heavy equipment. However, the postwar years brought two developments that would prove essential to Bombardier's continued success and to his permanent place in the history of invention and technology.

The first was economic prosperity. Suddenly, thousands of Canadians had money to spend on recreation. The timing was critical. Bombardier introduced his "Ski-Dog," or "Ski-Doo," as it was quickly renamed, onto the market at just the time when people could afford to buy such a machine, more often for the simple pleasure of whisking over the snow than for work of any kind. A booming economy helped to make Bombardier's name a household word.

The second crucial factor in the eventual success of the Ski-Doo was the rapid progress in small-engine technology brought about by World War II. Under the pressures of war, materials and virtually every aspect of engine design improved dramatically. Combined with Bombardier's track system and experience with snow travel and ski steering, the new small motors helped to produce the ultimately versatile snow machine. The single (and sometimes double) track of the new design meant that it could be steered by the driver simply leaning to either the left or the right. Its lightness and precise weight distribution meant that the machine could, in many cases, float over, rather than plough through, the snow. So sophisticated was Bombardier's vision that the snowmobile's basic concept, shape and design has never varied significantly from Ski-Dog #1, which Bombardier took north to James Bay for testing.

Any concern about L'Auto-Neige Bombardier's ability to survive the setbacks caused by the war was dispelled once the public discovered the little sled Bombardier had modestly hoped would be useful to missionaries, trappers, woodsmen and farmers. Sales increased by more than 100 percent for each of the first several years of production. Even as competitors jumped in with their own models, Bombardier had to find a way each year to produce more than twice as many machines as he had the year before. By 1965, there were over 50,000 snowmobiles in use, and Bombardier's company alone was turning out 15,000 more per year. The hardworking, sober-minded inventor from Valcourt, Quebec, had unintentionally precipitated the most exciting new winter sport the world had seen in centuries, and across the North American snowbelt, snowmobile clubs sprang up, sponsoring everything from leisurely day trips to oval-track competitions, rallies, sprints and marathon cross-country races.

For all his worldly success, Armand Bombardier preferred the quiet, full life he had created for himself in Quebec's Eastern Townships — spending time with his family, hunting with his friends, participating in community events and devoting the lion's share of his time to design and innovation. Blessed with a cool, practical business sense, Bombardier made every decision only after carefully weighing each option, all the while maintaining the strictest quality control in his own operation. While his machines took the Bombardier name around the globe, he rarely strayed from his hometown, and as his company prospered, so did Valcourt. Profits from the business flowed through the community. The village that had watched and encouraged its own eccentric native inventor grew into a small, prosperous modern city as Bombardier's snow machines found enthusiastic markets around the world.

Indeed, the groundwork Bombardier laid for his company was so

THE FIRST SKI-DOO, APRIL 1959

sound that L'Auto-Neige Bombardier was stable enough to survive and continue to thrive despite the death of its founder in 1964. Eventually, whole teams of research-and-development personnel were formed to carry on the work that Joseph-Armand had begun alone in his tiny Valcourt garage. The family business, made into a public company in 1969, has since expanded into almost all fields of transportation technology. The young man who wistfully studied aeronautical journals in his spare time spawned an empire that eventually provided parts for NASA's lunar modules.

But the real story of Joseph-Armand Bombardier is of the man who took his first snowmobile into northern Quebec to test it under realistic conditions and to hear the advice of those who would benefit most by its creation. Bombardier knew from years of experience how ideas and drawings translated into meshing gears and smooth-running machinery. His inventive imagination could turn flickering possibilities into new realities. But he possessed other traits as well. He did not simply dream wild dreams of wondrous inventions. He was a native of rural Quebec who saw snow travel as a problem and a challenge to be overcome. Neither fame nor fortune was as important as surmounting the obstacles he encountered, and surmount them he did, with persistence and enthusiasm. Rather than merely dispatching an eager employee or two to conduct the test trials of his latest invention, he went himself. A businessman who had built a hugely successful company, Armand Bombardier nonetheless saw his life in more practical terms: he bent his skills to the task of producing vehicles that would improve the lives of those who confronted rugged Canadian winters.

Success and wealth were not nearly as interesting to Bombardier as was machinery, how it worked and how it could be made to work better. By the time he had boarded his plane in northern Quebec to return home in the spring of 1952, Bombardier had a list of modifications for his new winter vehicle. Left behind with a local trapper was the prototype of the first modern snowmobile. The machine that sparked a revolution in winter travel and recreation eventually found its way into a museum; but first, it saw 10 years of the hard trapline use for which it was designed. That was the measure of Joseph-Armand Bombardier's success.

FURTHER READING

PROLOGUE

SAM SKINNER wanted to see me as soon as possible. He had been chief of staff for two and a half months, and we'd never met.

The West Lobby of the White House quickens the heart and loosens the bowels. Few visitors sit. They stand and talk nervously, eyes tracking each staffer who crosses the lobby at a near run. A member of the cabinet sweeps through with his nose in a document, impervious to the petitioners.

I gave my name to the receptionist. Smiling at Karl, the big, friendly usher, I glanced at the coffee table and saw that day's *Washington Times,* which carried yet another "story" attacking me as the government's official smut purveyor.

White House rules prohibit visitors from wandering in the halls, so a staffer is dispatched as a native guide to lead you to your destination. My escort, it turned out, was Susan Slye, the wife of Joe Slye. Joe had been the public affairs director of the National Endowment for the Arts — until I fired him. Susan left me at the chief of staff's door with a malevolent smile, saying, "And here's Mr. Skinner's office."

Except it was John Sununu's office — same couch, same fireplace, same wingback chairs bearing the same newsprint smudge marks from the former chief of staff's hands. I could almost see Sununu slouching there, delivering what, in my case, was always bad news. Only the nameplate had been changed to reflect the current occupant.

Sam Skinner greeted me, threw some logs on the fire, commented that his greatest disappointment of the 1990 election had been my brother Dave's loss in the Oregon gubernatorial race, and canned my ass. The day was February 20, 1992. I had lasted two and a half years as chairman of the NEA.

There were, of course, some preliminaries. He knew that I had talked with the president in October about returning to private life, and he said it had been the president's impression that I was going to leave within several months of that conversation. I confirmed that the conversation had taken place, and I added that I had contacted the president in January to say that I wanted to complete certain projects at the Endowment and if that was a problem, please to let me know. He had written back within hours, saying, "No problem" — I should simply contact him directly when I wanted to leave so that we could coordinate announcements to the media.

"When?" said Skinner.

"I was thinking August, before the Republican convention starts."

"That's unacceptable."

I told him about an arts and education partnership meeting that was highest on my agenda, a long-postponed trip to Japan at the invitation of the cultural leaders there, and a rural arts conference.

"When are those over?"

"The last one ends on March 31," I said.

"How about April 1?"

"That's a bit abrupt. How about giving me until May 1?"

"I'll check with the president and let you know this afternoon."

"I would like to delay the announcement until shortly before I depart so I will not be compromised in the projects I want to complete before leaving," I said.

Skinner was adamant. "It has to be announced within the next couple of days. Buchanan has fixed on this issue, and you don't want to be the favorite subject of that bully for the next six or seven weeks."

For the past two and a half years I had been the favorite subject of "that bully," in the form of Senator Jesse Helms, the columnists James Kilpatrick and Evans and Novak, Congressman Robert K. Dornan, and others. The faces changed, but the distorted, homophobic, and anti-intellectual attacks were remarkably the same. I could have cared less.

At least the cards were now face up, since Sam had originally told me that they wanted me to name the date I would step aside so they could have my replacement on board and confirmed before I left. Given the lethargy of the Office of Presidential Personnel in identifying and moving candidates through, that would have been a land-sea record. We left it that Skinner would talk to the president about the date of my departure and when it would be announced, and would call me later.

So out I went, unescorted this time, toward the West Wing lobby. At the end of the hall, standing in a foyer and looking as if he needed something to do, was John Sununu. Like giving a quick look over your shoulder in traffic when you realize that a lane change is not possible, I stuck out my hand and said, "How are you, Governor?"

"Hello, John."

Bookends: Joe Slye's wife and John Sununu on my last trip to the White House.

Larry Manley, the driver for the Endowment and my friend, drove me back to my office in the Old Post Office Building, between the White House and the Capitol on Pennsylvania Avenue. I didn't tell him I had been canned, but I think he knew it. The United States postmaster had once sat in my office. The high, ornately bordered ceilings still bear the U.S. crest. What is now a bathroom was the postmaster's vault, and the office is light and spacious, with a small sitting area in the corner turret facing the Washington Monument. I sat in my chair and stared for a while, taking my emotional temperature. *I'm fine,* I thought, but then I called my wife, Leah, and heard my voice cracking as I described the meeting. I experienced the same unintended modulations a few minutes later when I called Congressman Sid Yates's office and talked to tough, sweet Mary Bain, his long-time assistant. Yates was the patron saint of the arts in Congress; he had to be told.

Sam Skinner called later that afternoon. He had talked to the president and May 1 was okay. "Announce tomorrow," he said. I told my immediate staff: Beth Stoner, Keith Donohue, E'Vonne Rorie, and

Lisa Meredith. They set an all-Endowment meeting for ten o'clock the next morning, and I went home.

That night, like many nights — sometimes as many as six in a row — we had an Endowment-related function to attend. This one included a dinner and the opening of Molière's *School for Wives* at the Arena Stage. To the play's credit and my amazement, I enjoyed the performance, losing myself in the hysterical machinations of the jealous husband, Arnolphe, played with manic abandon by Richard Bauer.

Leah and I got home at 11:00 P.M., and I still had not written my farewell to the Endowment family for the next morning. So, as I had done so many times when preparing final arguments in the lawsuits I had tried in Portland, I got up at 5:00 A.M. and worked at the kitchen table. I reviewed the resignation speech I had drafted the previous October, when it had looked so certain that Helms's unconstitutional bill restricting arts funding to works with "approved" content would become law. Those remarks were dated. The emotions of then were different from the emotions of now. Indeed, the message was different, too. I wrote a statement of belief — a credo that would both define what I was and salute those who had worked so hard in the Endowment.

When I got to the office, I drafted a letter of resignation that simply said, "Dear Mr. President: Last October I told you of my desire to return to private life. Accordingly, I submit my resignation effective May 1, 1992."

About 9:15 A.M., Ede Holiday, the secretary to the cabinet, called. She had just heard at the White House staff meeting that I would be leaving. In her most solicitous voice, she asked if there was anything she could do to help. I demurred. Well, she wondered, could she see my statement? I said I would fax it over as soon as it was finished, along with a copy of my letter of resignation to the president.

She called back fifteen minutes later to say that my resignation letter was "awfully curt" and that it might "leave the wrong impression." She went on to tell me that when an agency head resigns, he usually takes the opportunity to brag about all the accomplishments of his tenure. I told her I had seen those kinds of letters and they made me want to barf.

"Yes, but it's typical," she said.

"Let's let history take care of it."

"Well, could you say something nice about the president, then?" she asked.

Pause. "Okay." And so the letter became

Dear Mr. President:

Last October I told you of my desire to return to private life. Accordingly, I submit my resignation effective May 1, 1992. I have appreciated the opportunity to serve you and the arts; you know how much your personal support has meant to me during these difficult times.

You and your administration have accomplished a great deal and I'm sure the best is yet to come.

In a request that reminded me of being told to dig your own grave before you're executed, Ede then suggested that I send over "some language" the president could use in his statement about my "resignation." As it turned out, none of what I sent was used in any recognizable form. The president's response later that day started, "Dear John, I received your letter of resignation today, and with sincere thanks and appreciation for your service, I accept your resignation effective May 1." He said he realized that the job was a tough one but that not all the art funded by the NEA had his "enthusiastic approval." The press noted that the president received the resignation without the typical expression of regret, and indeed, the spin doctors from the White House let it be known that I had been fired.

At 10:00 A.M. the entire Endowment staff gathered in Room M09 of the Old Post Office Building, one of the least hospitable spaces in a town of many architectural monstrosities. The room has a galactic ceiling, hopeless acoustics, adulterated architecture, and is, in a word, ugly. Since a presentation honoring Martin Luther King, Jr., was scheduled for later in the day, a podium, a mike, and chairs were already in place.

I looked out on the faces of my staff — good and dedicated and talented people. I said that art is essential to our lives and expresses our aspirations, pain, uncertainty, and joy. By supporting the arts without content restrictions, our government encourages us to dare,

for by the government." (Robertson would revisit the arts issue frequently in the next several years. His Christian Coalition verbally
assaulted homosexuals, and in a full-page newspaper ad he challenged Congress to "make my day" by reauthorizing the NEA and
the blasphemy and sodomy he claimed it promoted.)

But the galvanizing event came on June 12, when the Corcoran
Gallery, after sending out advertisements and invitations, abruptly
canceled the Mapplethorpe exhibition, stating that it did not want to
affect the Arts Endowment's congressional appropriation adversely.
The art world exploded. On June 16 the gallery, just across 17th
Street from the White House, was picketed by hundreds of artists.
Mapplethorpe photos were projected onto the outside walls of the
gallery during a candlelight vigil, and papers across the country carried the story on the front page.

Robert Mapplethorpe, recently dead of AIDS, had been a highly
visible figure in the world of fine art photography for several decades.
His stylized portraits and studies of flowers were praised by some,
dismissed by others. But his so-called X, Y, and Z portfolios, for those
who saw them, were hard to dismiss. Depicting the brutal and sexually extreme world of homosexual men in New York in the late
1970s, five photos from these portfolios that were included in the
canceled retrospective assured that the Endowment would be the
battlefield for a cultural war that rages on unabated as this book is
being written.

I was hopeful that Serrano and Mapplethorpe would be history by
the time I got to the Endowment and was determined that I would
not comment on either until after my Senate confirmation. Presidential Personnel suggested this same strategy, but not to the extent that
it was later used in the "know-nothing" hearings of the Supreme
Court nominees David Souter and Clarence Thomas.

Our best information was that the Senate would take up the confirmation sometime between the second week in September and the
end of the month. We knew that a single senator, out of pure cussed-
ness, could delay a nomination indefinitely, but we saw no virtue in
banking on that possibility and thus moved to sell our house, along

with a canoe, lots of furniture, two cars, and tons of other accumulated possessions too forgettable to list.

While we were busying ourselves with the mundane details of moving, our new life of controversy intruded. I received my first "chairman letter," in which a woman expressed her disgust at a "picture of Christ" submerged in a jar of urine. "This type of art would be repulsive no matter who was in the bottle," she wrote. Leah and I laughed and thought of a few visages for whom the medium would be appropriate. But the hostility of some religious people toward art was disquieting.

My life had been equally formed by the twin influences of music and religion. My mother insisted that all of us go to church as a family every Sunday morning. With the exception of an occasional fight after Sunday school, in which Ken Durkee would slug me in the stomach, church was a pleasant enough experience. Mira, four years older than I, Dave, two years older, I myself, and Phil, five years younger, all sang in the choir from my earliest memory. Grace was always said, sometimes sung, before meals, and on Sunday afternoons after dinner Mother would appear with the Bible in her hand and say with a small smile, "It's time for family worship," which in earlier years elicited groans and in later years some pretty substantial protests.

Four-part harmony within our family was commonplace by the time I was five. Phil, of course, wasn't around to join in then, but my mother did. Our living room contained two grand pianos, a Baldwin and a Chickering, which my mother and sister, and later Phil and Mira, played together. I started lessons in early grade school but wouldn't practice, being more inclined toward sports. (Medford High School's sports teams dominated the state, and I was named scholar-athlete of the year in 1960.) My mother told me I would be sorry if I quit piano lessons. She was right.

At Stanford I sang in the Memorial Church choir and studied voice with Ivan Rasmussen, although *studied* is not quite the right word, since my practicing was pretty much confined to vocalizing in the car on my way to a lesson. At the same time I was taking courses in the Old Testament, theology and contemporary literature, and the history of religion. The Stanford chaplain told me of a program that the Rockefeller brothers' fund had for people who were considering the parish ministry as a vocation. Successful applicants would receive one year's full scholarship to a theological seminary of their choice. I applied and was accepted, so I chose Union Theological Seminary in New York City, a nondenominational institution of the highest academic repute.

In the summer of 1962, as a volunteer in youth clubs in England, I came closest to what might be called "a religious experience." Tubby Clayton, the vicar of All-Hallows-by-the-Tower Church in London, was our leader. A legitimate hero who served as a chaplain in World War I, he founded the British equivalent of the YMCA, and on seeing that British tankers were being torpedoed and the crews had no chaplain early in World War II, he volunteered to start a chaplaincy corps on board those ships and made a dozen voyages himself. One night in the chapel he said he would give me a blessing, and as he laid his hand on my head and said a prayer, I came close to sensing God. But it didn't last, and like St. Paul, I have found faith and doubt inextricably joined in my existence.

Since divine intervention appeared unlikely, I decided I had better get on with it, so in 1965 I went to the University of Chicago Divinity School to sit at the feet of Paul Tillich, who was at that time exploring the relationship between Christianity and other religions. He had found, on fleeing Hitler, that when he changed from discussing theology in German to discussing it in English, not only the language but the theology itself changed. I heard his last lecture; three weeks after I arrived in Chicago, he suffered a heart attack and died.

Without doubt, my Christian ethics degree was helpful in my candidacy for Endowment chairman, since the White House made an unnatural obeisance to the fundamentalist right. But my theology, if anyone had asked, was a theology of inclusion. Religion, to me, has always been liberating. It is God that allows us to love and to understand and to forgive. Such, I would find, bore little relationship to the creed of those who bombarded the Endowment.

Although Donald Wildmon and Pat Robertson screamed blasphemy, Andres Serrano may have intended the crucifix in urine to be a statement against commercialized Christianity. A Catholic who had renounced the church, he had struggled with doubt and faith and with the role of religion in his life. He was experimenting with the use of bodily fluids — blood, semen, urine — in his photography. He disclaimed any intent to blaspheme, and when I conversed with him some months later, he indicated that the piece could be described as expressing disgust at the sugarcoating of the cross that contravenes its traditional theological significance as a depiction of man's inhumanity to the Son of God. When I asked why he hadn't made that point clear, he simply shrugged. He is, by his own description, not a man of words.

I first read of the controversy three thousand miles away, in Oregon, not yet the nominee but knowing I was close. Distressed at the fundamentalists' one-dimensional interpretation, I asked the Reverend Dr. William R. Long, the interim pastor of the Westminster Presbyterian Church and a former professor of religion at Reed College in Portland, for his views. Admitting that *Piss Christ* might be repulsive or even blasphemous, he said, "It also asserts that the cross, the very heart of the Christian faith, is itself an offense to God and human decency. Seen from this perspective, the work of Serrano may have the unintended effect of reminding Christians and others of the ignominy and repulsiveness of the symbol which they hold so dear."

After noting that we do not have to look to the artist for the definitive or even the controlling interpretation of a work, Dr. Long suggested that in Christian theology, the crucifix is a symbol of rejection and pain. Death by crucifixion was a slow, torturous process in which the victim's life gradually ebbed away as he was racked by the pain of the nails in his flesh, the loss of blood, and eventually suffocation, when the feet could no longer support the body's weight and the lungs could not gain breath. Sometimes the victim's legs were broken as an act of mercy, to hasten the agonizing death.

In our culture, said Long, the cross has lost its repulsive character. In contrast, urine, in modern parlance, is used as a test for truth: for steroids, drugs, and alcohol. He asked, "If we see urine as truth serum, does the crucifix in urine reflect some of the unyielding cruelty in human beings which we so desperately ignore or minimize?" Although Serrano might not have had any of this in mind, the result of the piece could have more to do with the interpretative power of the viewer than with the character of the artist. But Long cited Phillips Brooks, the nineteenth-century New England minister, who once defined his goal as a preacher "to comfort the afflicted and to afflict the comfortable."

Surely nothing in the indignation and outrage of Wildmon, Robertson, Helms, and D'Amato would suggest, in their wildest imaginations, that such a piece would provoke thought. Nor was such an interpretation within the realm of theological possibility in my conversation with the Reverend D. James Kennedy, a conservative religious leader from Coral Gables, Florida, some months later. His comment was "You couldn't persuade me of that in a thousand years."

Back in Washington, the House of Representatives began to debate the budget appropriation for the Endowment. The $1.5 trillion U.S. budget originates annually at the Office of Management and Budget (OMB) in the White House. It is formally presented to Congress in January and then lumbers through first the House of Representatives and then the Senate in thirteen separate bills. For reasons of historical accident, the Arts Endowment's budget is included in the appropriations bill for the Department of the Interior. In 1989, the Endowment appropriation of $171 million was part of an $11 billion Interior bill.

Since all revenue measures must, by constitutional decree, originate in the House of Representatives, a House subcommittee, after substantial staff work, calls witnesses and holds hearings on the president's budget (sometimes ignoring it entirely and substituting its own version) and moves the bill through to full committee hearings (where witnesses are not usually called) and then to the floor of the House. This process takes place over a number of months. During this time lobbyists for various special-interest groups review the legislation with the welfare of their constituents in mind. By the time a bill reaches the House floor, controversial issues have typically been aired in committee. Not so with the 1989 Arts Endowment's budget. The

Mapplethorpe and Serrano crises blew in like a Santa Ana wind — hot, suffocating, unexpected, and violent.

The House chamber is on the south side of the Capitol rotunda. When the House is in session, the American flag flies over the south wing of the Capitol, proclaiming to all who view it from the Mall that government business is under way. Electronic panels showing the names of all 435 representatives form a striking contrast to the traditional and stately gold clock above the flag that frames the dais and the chair of the Speaker. The chamber itself is rather plain, with rows and rows of brown leather chairs joined arm to arm and a slender-necked podium on each side of a round table from which either Republicans or Democrats can address the assembled body. Scoreboards like those in an old junior high school gym are found on the railings at both the right and the left, and in back is perhaps the most important implement of our times: the C-Span camera, which is sometimes the only observer as members address a chamber devoid of their colleagues.

But the chamber was far from empty on July 12, 1989, a week after I was nominated. Three amendments to the Interior appropriations bill were offered. Dana Rohrabacher, a freshman congressman from California and a former Reagan speechwriter, moved to abolish all funding for the Endowment; Dick Armey moved to cut 10 percent of the Endowment's funding; and Charles Stenholm, a Democrat from Texas, moved to cut $45,000 — the combined amount of the Mapplethorpe and Serrano grants — from the Endowment's budget. Congressman Sidney Yates, the Illinois Democrat who was the guardian and supporter of the Arts Endowment, had been persuaded that some concession had to be made, and he and the minority manager of the bill, Ralph Regula, from Ohio, had agreed that the Stenholm amendment would be it.

Rohrabacher argued that any government support of the arts was going to be censorious, but just to show that his argument wasn't bound by foolish consistency, he laced it with a litany of past horrors that the Arts Endowment had allegedly supported. He displayed his talent as a phrase-maker by saying, "Artists can do whatever they want on their own time and with their own dime," a phrase that would be echoed in numerous other debates in both the Senate and the House.

Then Dick Armey argued the hard line: "If you do believe in censorship — clear, precise, pinpointed, accurate censorship — you should vote for the Stenholm amendment. The Stenholm amendment says we want to exact a specific dollar amount in precise reprisal for these two specific art works. My recommendation says if you want an agency to act fiscally responsible as it husbands the money of the people of this country, then vote for stiff penalties and clear messages."

Ted Weiss, a New York Democrat, responded that the real issue was not fiscal responsibility but freedom of speech: "Ultimately, all three of these amendments take a piece out of America and what America is all about. This is basically a freedom of expression issue, no matter how one tries to disguise it. Mr. Armey, I think, is a bit disingenuous when he suggests that Mr. Stenholm is engaging in censorship with his $45,000 amendment but that he, Mr. Armey, is not with his proposal."

Armey rose to a point of order. He was offended that Mr. Weiss would label him disingenuous. In what passes for humor on the House floor, Yates wondered whether *disingenuous* meant pornographic. Weiss claimed that he didn't know that Armey was so sensitive and withdrew the word, then made some telling points: "There are other nations around the world which have standards for acceptable and unacceptable artistic expression. We call them totalitarian. . . . It is folly to argue that if federal funds are used for a project, that project must be acceptable to all taxpayers." He then quoted that great civil libertarian, former president Ronald Reagan: "'In recognizing those who create and those who make creation possible, we celebrate freedom. No one realizes the importance of freedom more than the artists, for only in the atmosphere of freedom can the arts flourish.'"

Reagan had said this during the presentation of the National Medal of Arts, an annual award that recognizes a dozen of this country's artistic giants. Of course, Reagan didn't write it and probably gave little thought to what it meant. People in the Arts Endowment recognized that each year they had one opportunity to write the president's words: his remarks during the presentation of this medal. Unlike most of their other testimony or public statements, these remarks were not fully reviewed by the OMB, and therefore they tended to be less equivocal. Unfortunately, although the president did utter such remarks in the Reagan and Bush administrations, little could be made of them, because they were the beliefs of neither the speaker nor the administration.

Armey continued to protest that his $14 million cut was meant simply to impose "discipline" on the Endowment for its past "transgressions" and that this was not censorship, whereas the Stenholm amendment was. Robert ("Call me Bob") Walker, a Republican from Pennsylvania, had a much more specific reading of the law that for twenty-four years had governed the Endowment without major political interference. He said, "The law in place says that you should not authorize an artist to urinate in a bottle and then stick a crucifix in it and call it art. That's what the law is all about right now."

In this first House debate, the points of view represented by Rohrabacher and Weiss were correct — that is, that the government ought to be either in or out of the business of supporting the arts and that there is no halfway position. Stenholm, however, while helping Yates and Regula to minimize the damage, made his point without equivocation: "Political pressure — you better believe it. To my colleagues who say there is no basis on this floor to have political pressure put on those agencies who depend upon us for money, I am here to participate in putting political pressure and believe that to be anything but censorship."

The Stenholm amendment passed, 361–65. Armey and Rohrabacher's amendments were defeated by similar margins.

The utter insignificance of the $171 million Endowment budget relative to the whole $11 billion appropriations bill should have signaled that a far more important issue was undergirding the three-hour debate on the NEA budget, which amounted to one two-hundredth of one percent of the annual expenditure of the federal government.

In fact, the controversial art fueling this debate cost each citizen a sum too small to calculate.

What made this attack on the arts different from periodic and short-lived earlier complaints against the Endowment — its funding of Erica Jong's *Fear of Flying,* the poem "Lighght" (that was the entire poem), and a children's theater group that urged the children to yell "bullshit" — was the rise of the organized right. Curiously, during the Reagan years, when getting for oneself was admired and promoted, the right wing also took control of values imagery. As selfishness succeeded, messages extolling "family values" began to be accepted, without analysis, as essential to order. As sexual and racial groups became more assertive, violence in the cities increased, and political and social groups focused on particular issues, such as abortion or school prayer, the cries for values from the far right wing resonated to greater and greater portions of the political middle. "Family values" often became a code phrase for exclusion, bigotry, and hate, and politicians, out of cowardice, ignorance, self-interest, or occasionally commitment, signed on to the fad without asking exactly what it was they were for, or what "family values" meant.

The far right knew, though. Homosexuality was a sin and was obscene, per se. Art should be uplifting, not challenging, and certainly not gross. This is a Christian country and God's word is revealed directly to the individual. Any art that uses religious symbols non-traditionally is blasphemous. And so on. Reinhold Niebuhr put this issue into perspective fifty years ago, when the morality of World War II was being debated: "Religion is so frequently a source of confusion in political life, and so frequently dangerous to democracy, precisely because it introduces absolutes into the realm of relative values."

To the far right, order was more important than freedom — in reproductive rights, the content of art, and behavior toward the flag. Not patient or confident enough to let the gritty conflict of ideas determine a winner, the right reached outrage with only the slightest provocation, and in Congress lawmakers sought to impose legislation limiting abortions, restricting blasphemous or indecent art (obscene acts have always been illegal), and requiring honor, or at least not dishonor, to the flag. As the nation slid into an economic depression,

lengthy argument, but I agreed in milliseconds. She had been the most dependable and pleasant associate with whom I had worked, and there was no one whose assistance I welcomed more. She could be a special assistant, troubleshooter, and lawyer for the agency. Her broad background did not include much in the arts — she had been a research biologist before becoming a lawyer — but her strong suit was finding solutions: getting things done and keeping me informed. She had saved my bacon repeatedly by bringing me issues and problems that needed my attention, and I trusted her completely.

Selina Roberts Ottum, a debutante from Philadelphia, had come west in the late 1970s to make a life for herself and her family in the decidedly classless society of Oregon. I first met her when she was running a local arts agency in Eugene in 1975. She subsequently became executive director of the Metropolitan Arts Commission in Portland, and through the 1980s so distinguished herself among her colleagues that she was elected president of the National Association of Local Arts Agencies. With good humor, a gentle touch, and a healthy degree of impatience, she moved the arts toward the center of local government in Portland and its surrounding counties. She had told me several years before, "We are taking over the world," and she had begun to promote legislation to require the purchase of art with a percentage of construction budgets for schools, public works, and other public buildings.

Selina and her husband, Phil, discovered that she had breast cancer in 1987. She underwent surgery, radiation, and chemotherapy, all of which were unusually invasive. But she was persuaded that she had been cured, and in the summer of 1989 she was anxious to work with me at the Endowment. No one was more qualified in the area of local and state arts agencies and public partnerships than Selina, and she was full of enthusiasm for building friends for the Endowment and partnerships with states, local governments, and businesses. I was cautious, for she had previously told me she wanted to spend more time with her husband and her daughters, then aged two and five, and I simply did not want to be the siren that lured her from that resolve. She assured me, however, that she and Phil had talked the issues over and that if I was interested, there was nothing she would rather do than go to Washington. Besides, she would be closer to her family in Philadelphia and Boston. I hired her without reservation.

I could see a team beginning to take shape, with Selina as a trusted ally in a critical role. Only when I arrived in Washington did I learn that, at least in the eyes of Presidential Personnel, I did not have authority to hire anyone without first getting political clearance. I told Jan that I had hired Julie and Selina, and within a couple of days she invited me to join her for a meal at the White House Mess.

The White House Mess is more or less under the Oval Office, down a narrow hall and a short flight of stairs and across from the Situation Room. Attended by stewards, it reminded me of being on shipboard, with dark paneling and no windows. The food is good, especially the desserts. One large round table stands near the entrance, and a scattering of smaller tables allow more privacy. The place has a special feel — it's for important people doing important business. But just to make it clear that this is not a classless society, the Senior White House Mess is separate, on the left of the hall before the stairs. That morning we were with the common elite.

When I arrived, Jan was sitting with Ron Kaufman, who described himself as the political purity official in Presidential Personnel. Kaufman was close to Sununu and was related by marriage to Andy Card, Sununu's deputy. All prospective appointments had to go through him for political clearance. He explained that Jimmy Carter's big mistake had been not to clean house and put his own people in. Kaufman was peeved that I had hired Julie and Selina, who were both Democrats. As if I were an errant child, he admonished me, saying that there were many people who had worked for George Bush for years and that they were going to get the remaining jobs. Only if I could prove that there was no one with sufficient Republican credentials who could do a job would he consider a non-Bush person.

I recognized that I was being wood-shedded and took it in good humor. But the net result was that even though I was in charge of one of the most visible and controversial agencies of the federal government, I was to be without the leaders to run the place for my entire tenure. One after another, my requests to hire the people I wanted were denied, and I was never allowed to have a full staff.

At that lunch I asked Ron Kaufman to help me shut down those Republicans who were using the NEA as a whipping boy and a fund-raising vehicle. Several days later he wrote me a note saying that he had talked with Republicans in Congress and they wanted to be *good team players* (his emphasis), and while accusing the NEA helped them make dollars, they would not do anything that would hurt my effort — "a point to be remembered when talking on the record about administration (our team) funding levels." I had transgressed as early as my confirmation hearing, when I told Senator Pell that our funding level was inadequate.

This was not my only introduction to how things operated in the White House. My first week on the job, I attended a briefing there for new appointees. Andy Card explained that the executive department could not lobby, but it could educate Congress, which amounted to the same thing. Both the president and John Sununu had open-door working styles, and while there was a chain of command, it was violated all the time. The president might call anyone at 7:00 A.M., and although he invited me to contact him directly, I was to find that any direct communication annoyed Sununu, who told me always to go through him.

Card said that Bill Kristol, the vice president's chief of staff, attended all briefings and was considered part of the president's staff. (On conservative issues Kristol carried Sununu's water, and thus he had a great interest in the arts.) Card told us that the OMB was the point of clearance for any testimony that we wanted to give Congress. Not only did the OMB have budget responsibilities, but it also assured that any policy going through an agency was consistent with administration positions. I was to find that the OMB staff and other employees of the White House acted as if they had never met. Consistency was not their hallmark.

Roger Porter, the president's adviser on domestic affairs, explained the Bush themes to us. First was realism. The president was willing to deal realistically with the problems he had inherited; for instance, sixteen days after taking office he had proposed a solution to the savings and loan scandal. Second was "kinder and gentler." Bush was interested in child care and the homeless. Third was investing in America's future. The president wanted to build a better-quality American life. The focus of the 1990s would be on learning to defer gratification and to make investments that would bear fruit for subsequent generations — increasing national savings and investing in the environment and education. What happened to these programs is a mystery to me. They were never heard from again, and to my knowledge, most administration actions were absolutely contrary to everything Porter said that day.

Amy Schwartz, from the White House legal staff, then explained the four principles of government ethics so that we would not run afoul of either the letter or the spirit of the law. Ethical standards, she said, should be exacting enough to give the public confidence, should be fair and reasonable, should be consistent across the three branches of government, and should not be unduly restrictive. Even though I had a master's degree in Christian ethics and seventeen years' experience in interpreting laws, after forty-five minutes of hearing slogans I had absolutely no idea what Schwartz was telling us, and from the looks on their faces, no one else in the room did either. While some claim that government ethics, like deliberate speed or military justice, is an oxymoron, certain principles should be both basic and understandable: telling the truth, not using government property as one's own, not ignoring procedures to benefit one's friends or achieve the administration's objectives. Plain talk was not the order of the day.

Ed Dale, from the OMB, said that the savings and loan bailout was "a wash, so it was considered off-budget." What? He explained how the deficit would be reduced over the coming years. He told us that our agency funds would be sequestered because Congress would not have finished work on the budget before the expiration of the fiscal year (which had already happened, two weeks before). The government was operating under a continuing resolution from the last budget appropriation, and the new budget was not apt to be resolved for some time.

I had just finished a lawsuit on accounting practices, and I had never heard sophistry quite like this: divorced from real dollars, from real accounting, and from reality, period.

FIVE

*I*T IS SAID that when artists form a firing squad, they stand in
a circle. I was ambushed on the way into Washington by the Artists
Space show, and I couldn't have handled it worse with a rehearsed
script.

Artists Space is a lower Manhattan gallery and artists' support
facility concentrating on emerging artists. Susan Wyatt, its director,
and Charlotte Murphy, the leader of the National Association of
Artists' Organizations (NAAO), apparently had cooked up a strategy
to provoke confrontation with the Endowment. To do that, Wyatt
contacted our museum program and then me, to alert us to "potential
problems" from a show the Endowment had supported, "Witness:
Against Our Vanishing," due to open in her gallery on November 16,
1989. The "vanishing" were people dying of AIDS. The show was
designed to commemorate them and to describe their suffering and
the perceived callousness of society's response to this plague. According to Wyatt, it contained photographs, sculpture, and constructions,
and there was a catalogue. The catalogue in particular was confron-
tational. It specifically mentioned political figures such as Senator
Helms and Congressman Dannemeyer.

The last thing I wanted was another controversy. We needed time
to let the dust settle, to figure out what the recently passed Helms
amendment meant and how to administer it. I sent Drew Oliver, the
program director for museums, who had had several years of Endowment experience, to New York on October 30 to look at the show

and the proofs of the catalogue. He reported back that the images were clearly explicit (that is, they whacked you between the eyes so you wouldn't miss the point), reflected anger toward society about AIDS, and had some nudity. Drew thought that a disclaimer was necessary, because the material was cruder and potentially more problematic than Mapplethorpe's photos.

The funding for this show was a 1989 grant that had been approved before I arrived. It was not subject to the new amendment, which applied to grants given after October 1, 1989, and the letter approving the grant had been signed by the acting chairman, Hugh Southern. I could simply have evoked the well-worn Washington device of blaming my predecessor, or, even more simply, I could have said, "I am going to act prospectively — what is past is past." (Leah could never understand why the Endowment professionals failed to counsel me against second-guessing this grant. She was not sympathetic.) Perhaps with a few months' experience I would have been wiser, but I was disoriented. My heart was in my mouth, and I felt that not acting, particularly when Susan Wyatt had dumped this steaming, writhing mess on my desk, would be a declaration of weakness. After all, an administrator is supposed to act, right?

I talked to Wyatt and Murphy on October 25 and again to Wyatt on October 31, at which time she told me she was going to print the catalogue with a credit to the Arts Endowment in it. I told her to put a disclaimer in the catalogue and to ask reporters, if they called, to contact me directly about the NEA's position. I was trying to find a compromise. Ironically, on October 27 Wyatt had written a letter to David Bancroft, a specialist in the museum program at the Endowment, in which she requested that the July 13 award letter be modified to exclude the catalogue, since she had found other funding for it (from the Robert Mapplethorpe Foundation). This letter was not received at the Endowment until November 7, and Wyatt didn't mention it; if it had arrived earlier, it could have been the basis for the compromise I was seeking. I'm not sure about Wyatt's motivations. She kept giving equivocal signals.

All we had at the end of October, in addition to Drew Oliver's report, was a rough copy of the catalogue of the show. It contained essays, a descriptive piece by the curator, and photos of some of the works. The most disturbing part of it was an angry essay by the artist David Wojnarowicz, who was infected with AIDS and was watching his friends and his society succumb to the disease. He attacked Cardinal O'Connor, of the Catholic church, for not taking a more compassionate approach to AIDS, and spewed his bile on political figures: "At least in my ungoverned imagination I can fuck somebody without a rubber on or I can in the privacy of my own skull douse Helms with a bucket of gasoline and set his putrid ass on fire or throw Rep. William Dannemeyer off the Empire State Building. These fantasies give me distance from my outrage for a few seconds."

On the morning of October 30, three weeks after my arrival, I called a meeting of about ten senior Endowment staff members in my office. All but one of the people at the meeting (Julie Davis, who had arrived a week before I had) were strangers to me. We dissected the Artists Space application to see if what the gallery was actually doing differed in any material way from what it had proposed. The application described the exhibition as focusing on sexuality, recovery from drug use, and death. The curator, Nan Goldin, argued that sublimation of sexuality through art was safe sex. "The exhibition will confront Goldin's ongoing fascination with sexual dependency as she perceives it in the work of contemporary artists." With language like this in the application and a grant award letter supporting the exhibition and accompanying catalogue "as outlined in your application," there was precious little room to quarrel about sexually explicit material. The gallery had said it was going to do it and the Endowment had agreed to support it.

The Artists Space application did say that the accompanying catalogue would include essays by art critics. Here there seemed to be a material difference, since the essays in the catalogue were by artists in the show. Some Endowment employees felt that if we did not distance ourselves from this show, we were "dead ducks." Most, myself included, were scared. Instead of freeing us from a summer of threats and intimidation, the diluted Helms amendment was a sword of Damocles, disabling us because it hung poised, not because it struck. The greatest threat seemed to come from Congress, and we needed time — time for other issues to divert its attention.

We discussed separating the catalogue from the show. I explained that I didn't want to annoy Congress further and suggested that if Artists Space would simply return the grant, we would all have the necessary breathing room. Susan Wyatt seemed anxious to accommodate us but made no commitments. She agreed that the catalogue was inflammatory. By this time Artists Space had a lawyer, and Art Warren, the acting counsel for the Endowment, and Julie Davis were talking with her.

Since the National Council on the Arts was meeting that weekend (this was my first introduction to its members), I mentioned the situation at what was supposed to be a purely social dinner on Thursday night, November 2. The council members around the table seemed to agree that the show was opportunistic, political, and inflammatory and that it wouldn't have been funded now. Some said that the applicant might have compromised the artistic quality by politicizing the show as it had. I told the council members that it was my intent to write to Susan Wyatt stating that the show violated the spirit of Congress's recent legislation, even though that legislation technically did not apply. My letter (already drafted) concluded that Artists Space should relinquish the Endowment's grant for the exhibition and print a disclaimer saying that the Endowment did not support either the show or the catalogue. No one at the dinner table voiced either caution or disagreement.

In retrospect, I see that this letter was hopelessly naive. Certainly neither the prevailing political climate nor actions in Congress that were thoroughly deplored by Artists Space and its adherents would persuade the gallery to relinquish a grant it had already received. Helping the Endowment was, in its view, making us defend the artists. Wyatt had to placate the most radical members of her board, and I was simply playing the shill.

The press, in the form of Allan Parachini of the *Los Angeles Times,* was sniffing a new scandal. Reporters cultivated their inside sources, and this conflict was reverberating throughout the already tender Endowment staff. By the end of the weekend of November 4 and 5, Parachini had talked to Susan Wyatt, knew that attorneys for the Endowment and Artists Space had had conversations, and knew that the Endowment wished to distance itself from the exhibition. His article quoted Wyatt as saying that while she regretted having to involve the NEA in a fresh dispute, she felt it was important for artists and arts groups actively to resist any restriction of freedom of expression. Parachini wrote that Wyatt's decision to warn me of the potentially difficult grant was part of a deliberate strategy to keep me from being blindsided by developments, but he also wrote that her tactics were intended to provoke a showdown over federal control of artistic content.

I called Wyatt and confronted her with this story, which she categorically denied. She told me that her board was meeting on November 6 and would decide at that time how to respond to my letter. She said that she thought we both had the same goal. So did I. She asked what our reasons for withdrawing support were, and I explained that the nature of the show had changed and become more political. Respect for individuals was one of my principles, I said, and this show was too inflammatory. Furthermore, at least one photo of masturbation was potentially obscene.

I hadn't seen the show, my First Amendment principles were in the lost and found, and I was simply out to lunch in trying to make a distinction between pure art and art that deals with politics. I knew I needed help, advice I could trust, but my problem was compounded by having lunch that day with Roger Stevens, the revered first chairman of the Arts Endowment and the former head of the Kennedy Center. I had asked him to share his wisdom with me, and over crabcakes with shell in them (I was told they were supposed to be that way) at Maison Blanche, near the White House, I struggled to hear what he was saying (he talks very softly and mumbles). What I got from that conversation, which reinforced my own muddled thinking, was that during the sixties, when Roger was chairman, the NEA tried to stay away from anything that was political.

Because of the *L.A. Times* article, other papers were speculating about "this delicate negotiation" between the Endowment and Artists Space. When asked by reporters, I praised Susan Wyatt for being responsible in talking about the issue with us. She was quoted as saying, "I wanted to offer them an opportunity, as it were, to kind of stand up for the show, to take credit for the fact that they funded it."

Wildmon got smarter and added the names of prominent advisers to the left side of his letterhead, which, at least on the face of it, gave more credibility to his organization. And the letters the AFA generated kept pouring in.

Congress didn't much care who was generating the mail. It reacted to citizen outrage with the knee-jerk response so characteristic of Congress generally, namely, by drafting some kind of legislation that would blunt the outrage. Fortunately, a virtue in a Congress of 535 members is its unwieldiness, which typically prevents quick action on anything and gives ideas of the moment a chance to sink of their own weight. A law prohibiting the Endowment from blaspheming would run afoul of both the free-exercise and antiestablishment clauses of the First Amendment. Likewise, Rohrabacher's proposed prohibition on the use of fetal material in artworks, in addition to being a solution for which there was not a problem, stretched the credibility of all lawmaking. The moral philosopher would argue that persuading one's fellow citizens of the rightness of one's view — by logic, or preaching, or even the venerable religious tool of guilt — is how one protects religion. Congress can't do it and shouldn't try.

The American Family Association's attacks were also effective because the group gained allies — the Southern Baptist Convention, the Eagle Forum, Concerned Women for America, Pat Robertson's *700 Club*, Focus on the Family, and others who recognized that the conservative agenda could be promoted by attacking the arts and making artists symbolize perceived license and immorality in American society. At the same time, mainline religions didn't just leave the field; they never suited up at all for this contest. (By mainline religions I mean the major Protestant denominations, the Roman Catholic church, and the Jewish faith.) My theory, which I roll out without claiming that it is more than an opinion, is that mainline religions were so invested in the civil rights struggle of the early sixties and the Vietnam protests of the late sixties and early seventies that they were exhausted and unwilling to engage actively in the social gospel or the struggle for social justice over the next fifteen years. Combined with their distaste for electronic evangelism, the growth and success of which left them voiceless, that meant that they simply weren't players.

I thought and asked and read to try to find someone in the religious world who could speak in defense of the Endowment. But leaders of the stature of William Sloane Coffin and Martin E. Marty, who were so effective in the sixties and seventies, just weren't there. I could not identify a single religious figure from the mainstream who could speak with moral authority for the principle of artistic freedom, which, after all, is guaranteed by the same amendment that protects religious liberty.

As luck would have it, some of the issues that I could have handled without moral or political hesitation were out of my jurisdiction. Take the case of Sniffy the rat, for example. Elizabeth Kastor, of the *Washington Post,* covered the Canadian artist Rich Gibson's plan to drop a fifty-pound concrete block on top of Sniffy, crushing him between two sheets of canvas on the steps of the Vancouver, British Columbia, library. Gibson said it would be a "thought-provoking work of art." Two directors of the Vancouver Humane Society announced that the concrete block would have to be dropped on them first, and the following day Sniffy was saved when the ecology group Life Force International confiscated the concrete weight from Gibson's car. Gibson was forced to flee to the safety of the Hotel Vancouver. He later returned Sniffy to the pet store from whence he had come, and Sniffy was subsequently bought (for $4.23, including tax) and presumably saved from being squashed or fed to a pet snake (which is the reason rats are typically purchased). Gibson was unimpressed. He thought that Mr. Hamilton, of Life Force, should have saved all the rats: "So I go, hmmm. I think, Mr. Hamilton, you're missing the point. You've been seduced by Sniffy's celebrity status. But I know that rat. That rat is just your standard rat."

Joyce Ziemans, my Canadian counterpart, had to deal with Sniffy, and I had to deal with Mapplethorpe and Wojnarowicz and Jesse Helms and screaming artists. Ziemans assured me that most of the problems the United States encounters float north in about six months. But she didn't have to run the reauthorization gauntlet with an increasingly angry Congress, and those hearings were less than a month away.

EIGHT

ON MARCH 5, 1990, the president sent me an "eyes only" note stapled to an image of Christ with a crown of thorns and a needle in his arm — a portion of a collage by David Wojnarowicz that had appeared in the Normal, Illinois, show. The president said, "I know you are as offended as I am by the attached depiction of Jesus Christ. I think you have been doing a superb job, so I send along this note not in any critical vein whatsoever, but simply to inquire if there isn't anything we can do about excessive cases like this." He asked me to respond directly to him, which I did, saying, "Yes, I was offended by both the work and the man, since I had encountered him directly at Artists Space where he was very angry and abusive toward me personally. Our original legislation, however, warns the Endowment to avoid imposing . . . a single aesthetic standard or to direct artistic content." I said that this was a wise policy, one that Helms and others were trying to tamper with and that we were defending with all our might. I couldn't bring myself to say — perhaps to acknowledge — that this, and other works, did not offend me. In fact, an image of Christ with a needle in his arm, particularly when he is not holding the needle, is consistent with an interpretation of Christ taking on the sins of the world — hardly a blasphemous concept.

American creativity, I said, needs some elbow room in which to flourish, and to put the kibosh on Mr. Wojnarowicz after he had produced the work would be unwise and would threaten our bipartisan support in Congress. Tightening up the panel process by assuring diversity, requiring panelists to articulate why any given application contains artistic merit, and making them aware of an artist's past work so that the applicant might thereby be accountable was at least part of the solution. I also recommended that the president appoint some excellent artists to the National Council, since he would have ten vacancies coming up shortly. (National Council members serve six-year terms.) We were recommending several qualified people to him, such as the symphony conductor James De Priest, the pianist Lorin Hollander, and the designer Maya Lin. I closed by saying that the Endowment had a tremendous opportunity to make this country a better place and to be a credit to Mr. Bush's administration.

That was Friday. The next day Leah and I escaped to Wintergreen, a resort in the Virginia Blue Ridge Mountains, for a couple of days, during which we hoped the Endowment would not totally dominate our lives. Wintergreen is allegedly a ski resort, but it can't compare to runs in the West such as Snorting Elk, at Crystal Mountain in Washington; Exhilarator and Saudan Couloir, at Whistler and Black-Comb in Canada, which are so steep that looking over the edge of them literally makes you dizzy; or even the bowls at Mount Hood Meadows, near where we lived in Portland. It was hard to imagine skiing here. Anyway, it was seventy-five degrees and beautiful — golf weather.

And the president called. The Camp David operator had reached my assistant Keith Donohue at the Endowment; he in turn called our home, and a workman who was there heard the message come in on the answering machine and decided that a call from the president probably should be forwarded. I called the Camp David operator back, and after being put on hold, hearing a number of clicks, and then being told, "Sir, this is not a secure line," there was the president.

"John, I got your four-page note, beautifully handwritten, which has been typed up for me as well, and it's a very sensitive reply."

"Thank you very much, Mr. President," I said. "It's an issue with which I have been dealing virtually every waking hour since I have been here."

"Well, I think you are exactly on the right track. I know you're doing everything possible, and I want you to keep up the great work."

"It's an extraordinarily tough issue. We are certainly trying," I said.

"I think you are doing it just right, to avoid the excesses on both the right and the left," he said. "How's the family?"

"Great. Leah and I are here at Wintergreen."

"Where's that?"

"It's in the mountains of Virginia somewhere," I said. "I assume it's near Camp David." I was hoping he would send the helicopter so we could nip up for a bit of tennis.

"Well, keep up the good work, and thanks for the reply."

I guess if you have to get a phone call while you're trying to forget about work, that isn't a bad one to get.

I learned from Patty Presock, the president's assistant, that Mr. Bush had shared my note with Sununu and had told Sununu that he thought I was exactly on the right track. Sununu apparently didn't agree, because he called me to his office two days later. When I entered from the secretarial area through the narrow mahogany double doors, the chief of staff directed me to the couch in front of the fireplace. He told me that the "obscenity thing" was a serious problem and that it could imperil the whole agency. Andy Card, his assistant, was there, but Sununu did the talking for all of us. On his feet, taking only enough time to bark out his orders before he was gone, he told me that there was a difference between public and private art (he didn't say what it was) and that we simply couldn't fund art that was political and only intended to get publicity. He said, "You at the Endowment only hear from artists; we are hearing from the rest of the world." This certainly was not the last time I would hear statements that separated artists from the rest of the world, or even artists from "citizens."

Insofar as I was allowed to speak (Sununu was on his way out the door before my turn came), I said that it would be helpful to have a public statement of support from the president — a notion that he did not dismiss out of hand. I also said that appointing eminently qualified artists to the National Council would be immensely helpful, since they would have the credentials to judge art on its merit and be relatively immune to claims that they were acting for political or personal reasons. He said to send him a list of names, which I did. (Nothing happened.) The rest of my agenda — our improved panel procedures, international opportunities, a national celebration of American creativity — was stillborn on my tongue as Sununu steamed out of the office.

I wrote a note to the president saying that he had been very kind to call and that as a small agency we sometimes felt isolated, particularly when we were taking fire from both sides of the spectrum. Sununu called that day to reiterate that the NEA had to "insulate [itself] from the statistical failures." I had told him when we met that the grants that were causing all the fuss were twenty out of eighty-five thousand the agency had funded over twenty-five years. He said that that didn't matter and that when he had been governor of New Hampshire, they had "simply taken care of it" (meaning that any artist who made trouble in New Hampshire was — what? Executed?). He said that I must repeatedly state my opposition to obscenity, that I couldn't say it too often. The following day, March 14, I sent Sununu a three-page list of quotes from news stories in which I had publicly opposed obscenity.

Meanwhile, Dan Quayle had been touring South America and had bought what the press described as "an anatomically correct doll." After three days of dry-mouthed dismay and confusion over why the vice president had purchased this lewd souvenir, David Beckwith, the vice president's press secretary, told reporters in a conspiratorial whisper that Quayle was on a secret buying mission for the National Endowment for the Arts. I ripped the story from the *Washington Post,* stapled it to a piece of my notepaper, and sent it to Sununu, saying, "First Rohrabacher and now this. How about some support for a change?"

Support actually came — in two installments. Literally hours before I testified on the reauthorization of the Endowment before the House committee on March 21, the OMB cleared our request that no content restrictions be included in the legislation. In my testimony I said, "After much careful thought and discussion, it is our conclusion that the legislation proposed here, which contains no content restric-

tions, will best serve the American public." My prepared testimony
included numerous procedural changes by which the panel process
could be made more accountable, such as adding an educated layper-
son to each professional panel. The primary thrust of my oral testimony, however, was to meet the criticisms of the fundamentalist right
head on.

After the obligatory statement that I opposed obscenity, I put in
evidence the American Family Association's full-page ad attacking the
Arts Endowment and pointed out its inaccuracies. I had pulled together the relevant documents about when Annie Sprinkle had per-
formed and when the Kitchen had drawn its funds, labeled them as
exhibits, and put them in a folder, and one by one I submitted them
as I would submit evidence in a trial. I had no idea whether this was
standard congressional procedure, nor did I much care, since I had
found that if you do something with enough assurance, it is generally
accepted as standard procedure. I said I had asked to appear on *The
700 Club,* Pat Robertson's show, because my answer to the criticism
was to supply the correct information and point out that what the
Arts Endowment had done was exemplary.

When I finished, Paul Henry, a Michigan Republican, and Pat Williams condemned some NEA critics for "duplicity and moral postur-
ing," Williams saying that they "believe that if they produce enough
lies at a fast enough pace they can anesthetize Americans to the
truth." Henry, however, opined that some content restrictions would
be necessary, and Thomas Coleman, a Missouri Republican, wondered how much the "chilling effect" of the Helms amendment had
really affected the arts community.

Other witnesses, including the novelist Larry McMurtry and the
theatrical producers Gordon Davidson and Joseph Papp, emphasized
the importance of the Arts Endowment (particularly one free of political interference) in encouraging young writers and poets. Davidson
pointed out that if *Driving Miss Daisy,* which had originated as a
stage play in a not-for-profit theater, had been subject to current
legislation, some moralist might have objected to the interracial relationship and sexual overtones and caused the producer to change the
play. Papp echoed the sentiment, citing the blockbuster stage hit *A*

Chorus Line, in which a character grapples with his homosexuality, a topic that could have offended some.

This was the second of three reauthorization hearings in the House. At the first hearing, held in Los Angeles (the home district of the chairman of the full committee, Augustus Hawkins), Pat Williams had wrung from me an admission that we might fund even offensive works, as long as they were artistically excellent. While he was asking these questions, I was thinking to myself, *Why are you doing this?* And indeed, that testimony was highlighted by the conservatives as a sign of artistic arrogance. The final hearing, in Washington, gave Endowment critics such as Dick Armey and Dana Rohrabacher a platform, but Paul Henry, to his credit, challenged Rohrabacher's demagoguery.

How well did our testimony work? It depends on what you brought to the debate in the first place. Some art supporters sent their compliments; for example, "It was honest, truthful, forceful, and made us all proud that you are the chairman." Another person said, "Your forthright, aggressive approach was brilliant, yet never combative." And a third wrote, "It is simply impossible to describe to you the sense of euphoria and excitement that was generated . . . by your testimony."

Lest one think that that was the entire universe, however, a Pennsylvanian wrote, "Please do not believe — even for a moment — that this nation is not disgusted, indescribably angry, and totally resolved to remove the NEA because of your incredible insensitivity, stupidity, and utter vulgarity." To the president, a Californian wrote, "To retain Frohnmayer in office, and to uphold him in his determination to open the floodgates of obscenity, is to open an official door through which these denigrators are given free license to traduce civility and public virtue."

Humor was not lost, as another man from California wrote, "I can't wait to get in on this wonderful scam and get some of that free money for the following art projects of mine. (Paintings are my speciality.) . . . Six highly intelligent dogs are shown peeing on all the past artwork sponsored by the NEA." And in the same urologic vein, a citizen sent us a jar of urine with a note: "I will be quite happy to

Within a couple of days of sending my note to Bush, I heard from two different White House sources that Sununu didn't like direct communications with the president. "Don't do it" was his instruction. But Andy Card called from Air Force One several days later to say that the president was firmly behind me, that what I said had made sense, and that he would respond as soon as he could. On June 19 the president wrote, saying that he too was troubled by all the furor. He didn't want censorship, but he didn't want a dime of taxpayers' money going to art that was "clearly and visibly filth." He said he was shocked by the examples in a recent *Washington Times* story ("describing," among others, Fleck, Finley, Hughes, and Miller) and that we had to find a way to preserve independence and creativity in the arts and at the same time see that taxpayers' money would not subsidize "filth and patently blasphemous material." "You are doing a good job and I support you," he concluded. In pen he added, "Keep it up!"

An apocryphal story recounts the dilemma of a man during the Civil War who could not decide whether to join the Confederate or the Union forces. Finally he put on a gray coat and blue pants, and both sides shot him. Search as I might for the middle ground, I was having trouble finding it. White House pressure to get out of the spotlight was increasing. Congressional pressure to accept content restrictions was increasing. The art world was nervous, divided, and disorganized. I was at ground zero, waiting for the detonation that would be my decision, pro or con, on the solo performer grants.

TEN

*E*VERYTHING IN Washington is political. I was a political appointee and reported to the president. The committees in Congress that were holding hearings on our reauthorization were made up of Republicans and Democrats, many of whom were openly partisan. That lawmakers such as Helms, Armey, and Rohrabacher were demanding information about specific grants from the Endowment made it clear that political attacks would continue. The General Accounting Office was now conducting several investigations of the NEA, which made us weigh our every action against political criteria. And the fact that Congress had reduced our 1990 budget by $45,000, the exact amount of the Mapplethorpe and Serrano grants, sent us precisely the message that Congressman Stenholm and others desired: we were the recipient of political pressure.

By early June the White House seagulls were flapping furiously. Three reauthorization hearings and one appropriations hearing had now been held in the House, but both our bills were stalled. Reauthorization was supposed to be passed before appropriations, to establish the framework for the agency. According to plan, the fireworks would take place there so that the appropriations legislation could follow unimpeded. But no one's plan was working. The massive onslaught of mail generated by the fundamentalist right had spooked even our supporters. Amory Houghton, for example, a New York Republican who was usually a solid arts supporter, was telling me to cool it — to keep the lid on.

Few in Congress saw the NEA as a defensible agency. Instead of praising the arts as a stimulus for economic growth (in sales and exports of books, recordings, movies, TV), as an integral part of education (teaching risk-taking, self-evaluation, and written, oral, and visual expression), and as a significant force in community building (encouraging tolerance, common goals, participatory projects), all they could envision was the two-second sound bite "My opponent voted for pornography." Seemingly, the First Amendment was a concept with which they were not acquainted. To defend the right of free expression, especially expression of unpopular ideas, got no votes, even though this notion is the bedrock of our freedom and democracy. Much more common was the attitude, most self-righteously expressed by Dick Armey, that artists were not showing proper respect for Congress.

In this context, then, Congressman Paul Henry was struggling to make a distinction between censorship and sponsorship — to come up with restrictive language that would not be unconstitutional. On June 5, Rose and I met with Andy Card and the White House's congressional liaison people to discuss Henry's distinction, which was, of course, nothing more than a slogan. The government is not the sponsor of any idea that is produced by an artist. The ideas belong to the artist; the government is merely an enabler. The government provides the soapbox, the artist the message. But I was perfectly willing to talk language as long as it was meaningless and would get Henry, the son of a conservative theologian, on board.

Since I would be appearing the next day before the Senate Appropriations Committee, chaired by Senator Byrd (this was an appropriations hearing, but reauthorization would be discussed), the White House wanted me to trot out the idea of a one-year, as opposed to a five-year, reauthorization, in order to give the independent commission time to do its work. (I did, but Congress showed no interest.) Why the White House had delayed so long in appointing its four commissioners and then allowed the clearance process to drag on I do not know, because the commission was a potential out for everyone: let it deliberate, make a report, and give cover to both Republicans and Democrats. As it turned out, the commission did substantially that, but in the meantime Congress didn't know what the White House was doing. Tom Coleman, the ranking Republican on the reauthorization committee, said to the press, "The administration reminds me of a car careening from one proposal to another." Pat Williams, the ranking Democrat on the committee, complained to a reporter that the White House was not communicating with either Coleman or himself, which "shows political naiveté and will result in serious political mischief." He opined that it could "allow John Frohnmayer and the NEA to swing slowly in the wind." That was the least of the White House's concerns.

Both Williams and Coleman were supportive of the Endowment, but they weren't talking to each other. Williams came from an academic background in Montana. His son was an artist, and Williams himself was an unapologetic liberal who believed in free expression, social conscience, and government as a positive force for change. He supported artistic freedom, opposed content restrictions unequivocally, and took on reauthorization of the NEA as a personal cause. Not hesitant to discuss strategy frankly with me (often while chewing on a cigar in his office), he was uniformly pessimistic about our chances of coming through without some form of content restrictions.

Tom Coleman had practiced law in Missouri before going to Congress. Rose DiNapoli had once worked for him, which should have given us an advantage in acquiring information. Not so. Coleman told us little except that he supported the Endowment and thought content restrictions were necessary, meaning politically necessary for him. Moreover, he had gotten it in his mind that more money should go to the states — another concept that was short on logic and long on political justification. With his large glasses, sharp features, and slightly boyish look, Coleman was never hostile but just sort of pissy, demanding that things be done his way.

On Friday, June 8, 1990, George Archibald reported in the *Washington Times* that Bill Kristol, Dan Quayle's chief of staff, was "leading the damage-repair operation on Capitol Hill." Acting on behalf of John Sununu, Archibald said, Kristol was mending fences broken by my intransigence in failing to accept "legitimate and necessary controls against federal support for the type of art the President has recognized as filthy and blasphemous." The story reported that NEA officials had been excluded from meetings on the Hill but that Kristol and members of his staff had met with Steve Gunderson, a Wisconsin Republican, and Dana Rohrabacher. The article also claimed that the White House was angry because I had not taken a firmer position against obscenity in a hearing (Senator Byrd's) before the Senate two days earlier.

I called Kristol to ask him about the story, and he said he hadn't talked to George Archibald. He apologized for what was said and promised to mention that he was annoyed with the story at the White House senior staff meeting on Monday. He didn't say it wasn't true.

On June 11, Andy Card told me that the administration had cracked the whip and there would be no more sniping at the agency or me by White House staff members. Such warnings reduced the gunfire for about six weeks, if that, and then the sniping resumed full force. Working in the White House, somewhat like being elevated to the lofty position of a judge, separates even normal and decent human beings from reality. Members of the White House staff often feel that in some sense they are the president, and thus can speak for him. The industry of leaking stories that attempt to position the White House on a particular issue has vexed presidents for decades. In fact, Nixon's plumbers unit, conceived to plug the leaks, precipitated his downfall.

The following week, Ede Holiday, who had just been appointed David Bates's successor as secretary to the cabinet, called me to say that a *Washington Times* story had triggered significant concern about art that was considered offensive. (This was the same story the president commented on in his June 19 note to me.) She wanted me to know that no one was interested in censorship but that there was a difference between censorship and use of taxpayers' funds — in other words, the rejection of controversial grants may *be* censorship, but please don't call it that. She hoped that in the future we could prevent such grants from coming this far — read, deep-six them early on. No one, from the president and his staff to members of Congress, ever told me to veto a specific application. But clearly lots of people were "concerned."

The next day I was called to the White House to meet with Andy Card, Bill Kristol, and members of the OMB and the White House congressional liaison staff to discuss the reauthorization. They told me that they wanted the Hill to solve the problem of what form the reauthorization should take, but that the White House would play a role in finding the solution. I was not to react to any proposal, and moreover, I was not to go to the Hill to talk to members of Congress without taking one of the White House staff members along. In short, I was grounded. The White House did not want to commit itself to a position before it saw what Congress was going to do. Its position was this: the Endowment's fate is in the hands of Congress; you, Frohnmayer, have nothing to say about it, and we're going to give you a babysitter to make sure you behave. The babysitter came in the person of Frances Norris, a perpetually sour woman who thereafter accompanied us on our increasingly infrequent visits to senators and representatives.

Nothing about this job was fun. The ever-present George Archibald wrote an article accusing me of forcing Endowment personnel to give me voice lessons and accompany my singing. In point of fact, we all had voluntarily enjoyed making music together, primarily for Endowment functions such as the annual recital and Hugh Southern's farewell party. Our common love of art — music, in this case — was what had brought us to the NEA. Archibald's accusations put an end to the singing and to much of the joy of being there.

What kept me going was my determination to succeed, both for the Endowment and for myself. The White House gatekeepers had taken away my special phone line, but I could use my regular line to continue to communicate with Pat Williams, Orrin Hatch, and a legion of other congressional leaders who were trying to find a solution to this emotionally charged problem. If I couldn't work with the White House, I would still try to solve the problem, with whatever allies I could find.

Although the members of the White House staff weren't much interested in my advice, they did solicit suggestions from the National Endowment for the Humanities about how the Arts Endowment could be tidied up, and they engaged in a little free-lancing as well.

4,309 letters of support and 1,367 letters of protest by the end of August. Both the Senate majority leader, George Mitchell, and the Speaker of the House, Tom Foley, refused to bring the reauthorization bill to the floor without an agreement among the members on the amount of time the debate would take. It had always been assumed that the House would lead the Senate in bringing a bill to the floor, a strategy that stemmed at least in part from the support the Endowment had traditionally enjoyed in the House. But this year, partly because so many representatives wanted to have a role in this legislation and partly because House members seemed to be running scared (all 435 were up for reelection), the Senate became the more promising venue for us. Senators Hatch, Kassebaum, Pell, and Kennedy had reached a fragile agreement under which obscenity was an issue for the courts, but if, after the final opportunity for appeal, a court found obscenity in a project supported by the Endowment, the Endowment would recover the money and the applicant would be debarred from applying again for some period of time. Staff aides feared that this coalition would dissolve over the August recess, but an even greater specter loomed: if the House did not act, it was likely that the Senate would not either, and the Endowment, without reauthorization, could expire.

Rose explained that some parts of the federal government had operated for years without authorizing legislation. Each year Congress would appropriate a budget and the agency would continue merrily along, presumably doing what it had always done. Dana Rohrabacher had already started to scream about such a possibility for the NEA, thinking it was a strategy by which the liberals would deprive him of an opportunity for confrontation. From my point of view, lack of reauthorization was the worst of all worlds, since it would prolong the uncertainty and the restrictive language we currently had. But my greatest fear was that people on the political left would conclude that government support inherently restricted free speech, people on the right would reiterate that the government shouldn't have been supporting the arts in the first place, people in the middle would fall out, and we would be gone.

Congressman Henry was still fiddling with language stating that the chairman of the Endowment would be required to ensure that any grant given was sensitive to the nature of public sponsorship and did not deliberately denigrate the cultural heritage of the United States, its religious traditions, or racial or ethnic groups. Additionally, the chairman would ensure that no grant violated prevailing standards of obscenity and indecency. How could I implement such requirements? To avoid deliberately denigrating the cultural heritage of the United States, would an artist be precluded from attacking slavery? Could an artist not speak out against religions that had promoted polygamy? Since obscenity and indecency were local issues, could the chairman ensure that every grant would sit well with every town in the country? It was a crazy time.

We were making a little progress with Congressmen Coleman and Gunderson, who still, despite opposition from their own state arts councils and virtually everyone else, clung tenaciously to the idea of redistributing the spoils to the states. We argued that many corporations looked to the NEA for guidance about where they might contribute; sending the money directly to the states would cut off that imprimatur. Redistribution would look inward at precisely the time in the history of the world when the United States ought to be looking outward, particularly toward eastern Europe, where communism was on the run and cultural diplomacy held so much potential. Moreover, we argued that these Republicans would be turning over more money to the Democrats, since most governors and mayors were Democrats. Local grants had always been subject to far more intense political pressure than those at the federal level, and such a plan would emasculate the federal leadership that had been so effective in creating media centers and literature programs and underwriting the salaries of folk art directors. One kind of leverage would be lost because federal funds had always been matched by the states, and states such as California, New York, Illinois, and Ohio would get less money in a formulaic redistribution, which made all the sense that giving equal cotton subsidies to Mississippi and Vermont would. Finally, state legislatures would be encouraged simply to decrease state appropriations in the face of such a windfall (and this is precisely what later happened).

The dumbest part of the redistribution plan, however, was that it didn't deal at all with the problem that had caused the brouhaha in the first place, namely, controversial work. Every controversial grant was already being matched by local dollars in the state where the performance or activity was to happen. Our grant guidelines required it. Coleman and Gunderson's bill was an example of legislators legislating because that's what legislators do, rather than of statesmen looking after the good of the nation. Tom Coleman told me in a moment of candor, "Pat Williams has gotten his publicity on this issue, and now I am going to get mine."

Meanwhile, we were working with Williams to try to find a Republican who could unify the Republican factions and work with the Democrats. Congressman Bill Goodling, from Pennsylvania, seemed a likely prospect, and he was willing to play the role. Williams cautioned, however, that the Democratic leaders would not accept a Republican bill. It had to be a joint effort, with assurances from both sides that the leaders of both parties would support a compromise. I negotiated with Coleman, Gunderson, the Texan Steve Bartlett, Goodling, and a dozen others to try to find the magic formula that would lead to a bipartisan solution.

Pat Williams's staff explained to me that if we couldn't come up with a bipartisan bill, there were three "trees" involved in this legislation, which might have to be voted on separately: the administrative changes to tighten up our grant-giving procedure, obscenity, and restructuring the Endowment (the redistribution issue). I also learned of a curious procedure called "king of the hill." This rule provides that the last amendment passed is the controlling amendment, superseding everything that was passed before it. For a congressman seeking political cover, the beauty of this procedure is that if a bill outlawing smut, for instance, comes up first, the congressman can vote for it and tell his constituents he has bashed obscenity, knowing that a subsequent amendment will undo his vote. It was a risky rule, Williams's people told me. I could think of a few other adjectives that would apply.

After long discussion, some of the arts groups that had been most adamant against giving any more money to the states were beginning to see that a compromise was necessary. Rose or I talked with them almost daily. They simply didn't want us to play that card until absolutely necessary. We were getting help from the AFL-CIO, both through lobbyists and through appeals for letters to Congress in the various union publications. Likewise, the U.S. Conference of Mayors approved a strong statement supporting the Arts Endowment without content restrictions, as did the American Bar Association, thanks to the information Julie Davis had given it. Even the American Family Association helped us out by making a scurrilous attack on Senator Hatch. As a result, the Salt Lake City paper, which had often opposed Hatch, issued a stirring editorial endorsing him and his stand on the Arts Endowment. Hatch redoubled his efforts to find a solution.

Several sophisticated arguments were emerging. Arthur Levitt, the former chairman of the American Stock Exchange, wrote in the June 28, 1990, *Wall Street Journal* citing the important lessons business could learn from the National Endowment for the Arts. U.S. corporations that are losing in global competition, he pointed out, concentrate on the short term and the bottom line, jettisoning research and development and risk-taking. Companies that succeed, in contrast, have much in common with the NEA. They are driven by top-line thinking: quality comes first. Second, they promote research and development, just as the NEA supports young artists who become the Alice Walkers, Billy Taylors, and August Wilsons of the future. Third, the NEA has not shied away from risk-taking and experimentation. The Vietnam War Memorial, the Dance Theatre of Harlem, the Calder sculpture in Grand Rapids, Michigan, and hundreds of other examples, now thoroughly accepted and loved, were criticized or doubted in their infancy. Finally, Levitt said, the arts and economic vitality appear to be linked in powerful ways, since many of the best places for business growth are communities that support cultural institutions.

Levitt might also have added a point made by Norman Cousins: making art infuses society with an incredible jolt of energy. This is the kind of value that economists try to quantify in nonmonetary terms. Art compels us to store ideas and dreams and possibilities, like a long-life battery. When we need them, scores of years later, these thoughts and dreams may emerge to illuminate people's lives. This is not the kind of energy that can be easily measured, but neither can much of what is taught in a liberal education.

The participation required by arts education — the discovery that "I can" — transforms children from spectators into participants in life, and in democracy. Similarly, the willingness to take risks and to make oneself vulnerable leads to growth and the ability to recognize and distinguish between success and failure. Moreover, art helps us appreciate our earth and its most amazing inhabitants, our fellow human beings. It is the confidence to take a piece of common clay and spin it into a bowl or to pick up a stick of charcoal and capture form on paper that helps us put value on our existence. With an instrument that is no more than wood and plastic, a musician can release the voice of the soul. This has to energize society. And perhaps this energy can help us relearn what the most primitive artists painting in the caves of Lascaux knew: that the art depicting the hunt and the hunt itself are inextricably bound in the process of human survival.

Art also helps energize our society by linking what has gone before, the immediacy of our present, and the dark glass of our future. The most profound wisdom of past generations is preserved in the arts — in painting, sculpture, architecture, music, literature, and dance. And finally, art energizes society because it makes more room in our minds. It allows and invites us to make connections. For the artist, nothing is impossible. No combination of materials is inappropriate. No flight of fancy is too daring. No combination of words is without possible meaning. And no thoughts are too dangerous to think.

By late summer, the great cultural giant was beginning to stir, although the only place where we were clearly winning was on the editorial scorecard. By July, sixty-five papers, along with *Time, Newsweek,* and *U.S. News & World Report,* had endorsed the Endowment and opposed content restrictions. Only eight papers, including the *Washington Times,* opposed us.

Some positive stories were beginning to appear in the newspapers as well. The *Christian Science Monitor* ran a story about a descriptive video service, which the Endowment had helped support, on a public television station in Boston. Descriptive video is a service for the blind, just as closed captioning assists those with hearing difficulties. In this service, a professional narrator describes the action on such television programs as *Mystery* when the actors are moving without speaking. The *Star Tribune* in Minneapolis featured a story on July 22, 1990, headlined "Whitney Bridge One Reason to Thank NEA." In Minneapolis, the NEA helped make possible a pedestrian bridge that links two parks and two neighborhoods separated by fourteen lanes of freeway. "For this achievement alone the public should be grateful," the story said. "But this bridge between Loring Park and the Minneapolis Sculpture Garden is much more. It is poetry in engineering," like the Eiffel Tower in Paris. The project was launched with a $55,000 NEA planning grant, which helped leverage a total of $1.6 million in other funds.

On July 24, *USA Today* profiled five artists who had received NEA grants. One of these was a metalsmith from South Carolina who was working on a piece of public art. The second gave credit to the Endowment for a literary center in Wisconsin that helped young writers. A Pima Indian weaver in Arizona, a playwright in Utah, and the Joffrey Ballet in New York City were aided quietly and effectively by grants. There was no mention of homosexuality, foul words, or nudity for a change. As Garrison Keillor had said in his congressional testimony in support of our reauthorization, "Forty years ago, to have an artistic career you got on the train to New York. . . . Today you can be a violinist in North Carolina, a writer in Iowa, a painter in Kansas. The Endowment has changed the way we think about art."

When humor started to surface, I began to have hope. In mid-August, the "guerrilla artist" Robbie Conal paid for a billboard in Los Angeles that depicted the face of Jesse Helms on a painter's palette, over the slogan "Artificial art official." When the sign went up, the subsidiary of 3M Company that owned the billboard took it down and then, a few days later, put it back up. Conal said, "I guess that the 3M national executives in their central office found that old crumpled copy of the Bill of Rights buried under the papers on their desks and . . . reconsidered." *Doonesbury*'s creator, Garry Trudeau, made one of his characters a performance artist who was concerned about getting a grant from the Arts Endowment on the one hand and self-censoring on the other. She had a bucket on her head and a rope around her unclad body. Dozens of other cartoonists across the country found the controversy fertile ground, and their humor helped to diffuse a bit of our critics' neck-vein-bulging righteousness.

Finally, we were able to place some articles or interviews in publications that would reach a wide audience. *Prime Times,* a publication of the Maturity News Service, wrote an article on the Endowment and its activities with older Americans, and *Christianity Today* carried an interview in which I attempted both to explain what the Arts Endowment does and to show how the First Amendment protects both religion and the rights of the speaker or artist.

Suddenly I was okay. In August Leah and I drove to northern New York and Vermont for a week's vacation. It wasn't our usual vacation — ski ourselves to exhaustion, play tennis until we dropped — but we had lots of time together in the car to talk, and for the first time since taking the job, I felt — well, that it would be all right, and that both I and the agency would emerge on the other side. Nothing about the trip compelled this conclusion. The 1981 diesel refused again, this time developing a problem in the electrical system. So we drove to Lenox, Massachusetts, the home of the Tanglewood Music Festival and the nearest car dealer. We thought about going to Tanglewood that night, which would have been a mistake, since the Boston Symphony held a three-minute protest against the NEA. Or was it for the NEA? It was getting hard to tell.

But when we returned to Washington, to find that a colossal car accident had wiped out thirty-five feet of our wrought iron fence, I was renewed enough for the fourth-quarter NEA reauthorization game.

TWELVE

*W*HEN I HAD SAID to the Endowment's program directors in late June that each of us had to distinguish between private and public morality and that I was going to have to do some things as chairman that I would not have done as a private person, what I was really saying, I suppose, is that one's ability to act in any given situation is proportionately constrained by the number of masters one serves. All masters can't be served, at least not at the same time. Choices have to be made. As a public servant, I could not complain about having to make such choices, any more than a Marine can complain during wartime that folks are shooting at him.

So, starting with the proposition that the Endowment deserved to survive, the questions for me in September were how could I best assure that survival, and whose expectations should I seek to fulfill, when, and for how long. The White House was the easiest of my masters, since the administration only wanted the problem to go away. There, the trick was to look as if I were a good soldier while charting my own course, having as little to do with the White House as possible, expecting no help, and avoiding getting fired if possible.

Next easiest were the taxpayers. Our job was to craft convincing arguments about the benefits of the arts to society and to make the statistics available. The rest of the education and lobbying process was up to the support groups: NASAA, NALAA, the American Arts Alliance, museums, labor unions, and dozens of other sympathetic and interested organizations. Labor unions in particular played a critical role, since they had a vested interest in the continued good health of the arts in terms of jobs for stagehands and electrical workers as well as professional writers, actors, and musicians. But equally important was the broad constituency they brought into play. Labor support helped blunt the criticism that the Endowment was elitist, and the intimidating specter of being "against labor" may have dissuaded a few members of Congress from bashing us. Moreover, Jack Golodner, the AFL-CIO's chief congressional liaison, was as savvy a political operative as any in Washington. To try to motivate all these groups, I traveled and spoke as often as I dared to be away from my office.

The radical artists were the hardest to enlist in the cause of reauthorization. Absolute, shrill, and unyielding, they were the least help for the task at hand. The phrase "arts community" is an oxymoron. Disorganized by its very nature (the creation of art is often a solitary activity), the art world was also incredibly divided in its opinions on what should happen to the Endowment. The most radical artists thought that the NEA's demise would be a good thing, perhaps on the theory that it would spring reborn, in a purer form, from the ashes. That theory, as one Endowment staffer put it, was from dream city. Other artists were looking to protect the 99 percent of the Endowment's work that was not controversial and thus were willing to cut the radicals loose, by accepting content restrictions if necessary. Many artists and arts groups had difficulty defending Mapplethorpe's most sexually graphic work but knew that content restrictions would cripple the artistic process; they never progressed beyond the handwringing phase. Trying to unify the art world was a task that had to be deferred.

That left Congress and one nagging question: why was I doing this job? As Jim Lehrer said to me in an interview, after enumerating the groups that were shooting at me from every angle, "You can't be enjoying this." Obviously not. I kept going because the Arts Endowment was worth saving, because I didn't want to fail, and, I guess, because I didn't know what else to do. I was in the middle of the swamp and any path out was treacherous. I wasn't a bumpkin any-

chamber to keep the Endowment alive and an appropriations bill in each to give it a budget, the chance of getting hit with some restrictive language was substantial. The final push came in late September. I was busy, particularly in visiting and talking with committee members to make sure they understood the Hatch bill in the Senate and the emerging Williams-Coleman compromise in the House. Rose and I visited at least twenty members in each house and phoned hundreds of others during late September and early October.

But we weren't the only ones working. Twenty-two conservative "pro-family" organizations formed a coalition and sent letters to members of Congress endorsing Rohrabacher's amendments. Phyllis Schlafly's Eagle Forum, Pat Robertson, Concerned Women for America, Paul M. Weyrich's Coalition for America, the Christian Life Commission of the Southern Baptist Convention, and the National Association of Evangelicals signed on to this effort, and Rohrabacher regaled them with the latest NEA outrage, the Mac Wellman play, which still was not funded by the Endowment and which Rohrabacher apparently hadn't seen or read either.

The White House, striving to win the Millard Fillmore award for courageous leadership, issued a statement that it was "intentionally holding off on taking a public position on this politically touchy matter until Congress acted." Clearly, the president was not going to revisit this issue. The real horse pill, however, came from alleged Republican leaders. Bruce Eberle, a Republican direct-mail consultant who had sent out several million solicitations that criticized the Endowment, said, "It's been a good issue, and the longer it stays around, the better." Ed Rollins, now the cochairman of the National Republican Congressional Committee, said the issue had "been a good fund-raising tool because you can take extreme examples of government waste and explain it to the people." Even if the Endowment had funded a hundred controversial grants in the past year, the "waste" would have cost each taxpayer less than a penny. What was most distressing about this direct-mail fund-raising was the contempt it showed for the American people. These Republicans knew they were "putting on the rubes" and did it without hesitation. I wondered whether I could remain a Republican. Moderate and liberal Republicans have a long and noble history of service in Oregon, but in Washington the species was nearly extinct.

In late September, the House Appropriations Committee recommended a budget of $180 million, a $9 million increase, and turned back, at the urging of Sidney Yates, a proposal by Tom DeLay (R, Tex.) to cut all funds for the Endowment until Congress passed a reauthorization bill. The conservatives were still afraid that the NEA would slide through with an appropriation and they would miss their opportunity to strut and preen and foam at the mouth for decency and order. Yates's strategy in the appropriations proceedings was to urge deferral of all content-restriction proposals to the reauthorization debate. Accordingly, Ralph Regula withdrew his amendment calling for "appropriateness for general audiences" but reserved the right to offer it again during the reauthorization debate.

Finally the day arrived. October 11, 1990, found the House ready to debate, the galleries full. Our vote count was still imprecise, and we were worried. The real test came on Rohrabacher's multipurpose amendment urging content restrictions for everything from flag desecration to the use of fetal material in art. Sidney Yates pointed out that in spite of eighty-five thousand grants, all the NEA's opponents ever talked about were Mapplethorpe and Serrano, as if the grants for their work were the only two the Endowment had ever given. Tom Downey argued that the far right had lost its Communist bogeyman and the arts had arrived just in time. On the other side, Ron Marlenee, a Republican from Montana, perhaps foreseeing that he and Pat Williams would square off one day for state office, opposed the Williams-Coleman compromise, saying, "The legislation before us is a smokescreen that lets junkies peddle their depraved sadistic wares." And Robert Walker strutted and sputtered, trying to show the Mapplethorpe photos for the C-Span cameras. With all the digging into our records that Rohrabacher and others had done, I expected a new parade of horrors, or at least some stirring oratory, but from the perspective of an admittedly partisan viewer, when they got to the party they didn't know how to dance.

Rohrabacher's amendment failed, 249–175 — a comfortable margin. Philip Crane, the host of the Acorns meeting I had attended the previous fall, apparently had forgotten his offer to "do anything he could for me": he proposed what would become an annual motion to abolish the Arts Endowment. Fortunately, his colleagues beat him like a rented mule, 361–64. Finally, the Williams-Coleman compromise passed overwhelmingly, 382–42. The following week, on October 16, the NEA appropriations bill sailed through the House, 234–172. Congressman Regula offered his content-restrictive language after all, and was defeated.

We were amazed. After all the sound and fury, all the hard work and the seemingly hopeless odds against us, support for the Williams-Coleman compromise was nearly universal. And yet I felt no euphoria. The process was only partly finished, and there was no time for celebration.

What one part of Congress giveth, another part of Congress can taketh away. The next day, October 17, the Senate Appropriations Committee undid much of what the House had struggled so mightily to do, largely through the efforts of a one-person wrecking crew: Senator Robert Byrd. In subcommittee, Byrd defied the entreaties of Senators Pell, Kennedy, Hatch, and Kassebaum, jettisoned their carefully prepared amendment, and in its place put the previous year's Helms language. He also reduced the NEA's appropriation by $5 million and inserted a passage requiring grant recipients to sign a pledge of compliance with the content restrictions. Byrd wasn't shy about using power; as chairman of the Appropriations Committee he controlled every senator's pork, and he didn't hesitate for a moment to substitute his own opinions for his colleagues' work. Undeniably well read, Byrd had little use for contemporary opinions, particularly those of his colleagues. His staff was scared to death of him, and he had a reputation for vindictiveness and petty vanity.

Byrd's unilateral actions in the Senate caused us severe problems. The "loyalty oath," which I had hoped a court would invalidate, appeared likely to land right back in my lap, since Byrd had included it as part of the appropriations legislation. Rose told us that Senator McClure did not like the idea of legislating on an appropriations bill (they do it all the time in the Senate, although the rules prohibit it). But McClure would not oppose Byrd. Bennett Johnston and Thad

Cochran, the southern senators on the committee, said that they would wait until the conference committee to challenge Byrd, but they were positive that he would not change his mind. It looked as if we would have to rally support to take on Byrd on the Senate floor. After I asked Senator Hatfield to talk to Byrd, we divided up the senators to call — to educate them, of course.

The day after Byrd's blitzkrieg, Tom Scully told me that considering how Byrd and McClure had worked me over at our appropriations hearing, he was surprised that Byrd had not done more. He thought I ought to take my lumps and sit down with the senator after the appropriations bill had passed the Senate. "There is no way to roll Byrd on an appropriations matter," he said. "On the Clean Air Act, the administration, Senator Mitchell, and all of the Democratic leadership went against Byrd, and we only beat him by one vote." This was advice I was not prepared to take.

I called Senator McClure and heard his justification for supporting Byrd in committee: the $5 million cut was a compromise to head off massive cuts; the restrictive-language debate had gone "around and around," and he and Byrd thought that restating last year's language would do less damage than anything else. McClure agreed with the passage mandating that grantees sign an affidavit (the oath). He said that no one had made a deal with Helms or with anyone else to guarantee that this language was enough or that Helms would be satisfied by it. McClure acknowledged that Byrd had a well-known and oft-stated opposition to anyone's legislating on appropriations bills (except, apparently, himself), and it was hoped that he would use that argument to head off any amendments from Helms.

During my tenure at the Endowment, I often found that those who did us the most damage did so under the justification of helping us by "preventing worse language." In the military it would be called friendly fire. One ends up just as dead.

Pat Williams explained to me that many unanimous consents are required so Congress can adjourn; one house cannot do so independently. "I am not willing to have bled politically all over Montana, to have both of my arms cut off politically, and let the Senate dismiss this matter with ten minutes of discussion," he said. "I will sit on the floor till midnight if I have to to get their attention." Meanwhile,

Rose told me that the staff members for Senators Hatch, Pell, Kassebaum, and Kennedy had met and agreed that something ought to be
done when the appropriations bill went to the floor, so they were
gathering support.

On October 19 we learned that Helms would offer four amendments when the appropriations bill went to the Senate floor: one
about flag burning, one that would transfer all of the interdisciplinary
arts money to arts in education, and two that were undisclosed.
Senator Coats might have an amendment (which would be negative),
as might Senator Lott (also negative), and Senator Rudy Boschwitz,
a Republican from Minnesota, was proposing an amendment to increase our funding! On October 21, Senators Helms, Lott, and other
members of the conservative cadre of the Senate met to discuss the
Endowment issue. Soon thereafter Senator Hatch's staff called to ask
what I thought about adding diverse religions to the criteria for
selecting members of the panels. I said I thought it was a very bad
idea, one that might be contrary to the establishment clause of the
First Amendment.

After what seemed an eon (the Senate was laboring over the armed
services bill), the Endowment appropriation reached the floor, on
October 24. This was the only chance the Senate would have to
debate on this issue — the reauthorization bill was still hostage to
Helms's threat of a filibuster, and the senators were clamoring to
adjourn. The debate pitted two Republican conservatives against each
other, Orrin Hatch saying that Congress could not effectively manage
matters that were inherently subjective and Helms railing against
"slime and sleaze." Helms did not filibuster, but he threatened to continue his arts bashing, saying, "Assuming that I am in the Senate next
year, which is up to the good Lord and the people of North Carolina,
you ain't seen nothing yet." The first of Helms's amendments would
have broadened the definition of obscenity by prohibiting projects
that "depict or describe in a patently offensive way sexual or excre-
tory activities or organs." It was defeated, seventy to twenty-nine.
(This same language, the following year, was approved by almost the
same margin, a phenomenon that Congressman Fred Grandy, a Republican from Iowa, called "character flow.")

As we held our breath, the amendment that Senators Hatch, Pell,

Kennedy, and Kassebaum had drafted undid Byrd's work. It essentially substituted postjudicial review for the Helms language, and it passed, seventy-three to twenty-four. At last we exhaled. Byrd had been rolled, not by a little but by a lot. But Helms, used to being the lone battler, kept on proposing amendments as senators drifted from the floor. He allowed as how it was all right with him if a voice vote was taken on his proposal to limit grants to artists who earned less than a certain income. It failed. I leaned forward as I watched on C-Span. Here was the great intimidator, who required roll-call votes so his minions could excoriate those who voted against his crusades, and now he was welcoming a voice vote?

Helms's motives quickly became apparent. The technique had worked the previous year, when his late-night amendment before a nearly empty chamber had given us the first content restrictions, and it worked again this year. Helms proposed that the Endowment prohibit grants for works that "denigrate the objects or beliefs of adherents of a particular religion," and this amendment passed by a voice vote. Less than a quorum was present, but no one asked for a roll-call vote. Later Senator Howard Metzenbaum said, "You just cannot leave Helms alone on the Senate floor."

The House and Senate went into conference almost immediately, with the prediction that the new Helms amendment would be dropped. Time and fatigue were at the table too. The members of Congress were exhausted from their bruising budget wrangle with the White House. Every issue seemed contentious, those running for reelection were anxious to return home for last-minute campaigning, and most were plainly sick of the arts issue. All along we had hoped that the least desirable portions of the Williams-Coleman compromise would be moderated in conference. Negotiators on the conference committee felt, however, that either the whole Senate bill or the whole House bill would have to be passed, and since the House bill both appropriated and reauthorized the Endowment, thanks to Yates, who had attached the whole House reauthorization bill to the appropriations bill, ultimately it prevailed. The grant-giving language it contained required us to choose grantees on the basis of artistic excellence, taking into consideration general standards of decency

After the Artists Space controversy, its November 17, 1989, head-line had been "Mr. Frohnmayer's Fumble." On March 2, 1991, an editorial was entitled "The Frohnmayer Fumble," and gratuitous it was.

The editorialist, Mary Cantwell, who had been out of the country, it seemed, during the entire two years of congressional debate, de-scribed the Helms language as "mild but tricky." She then went on to say that I was "out-Helmsing Mr. Helms at the same time [I] was preaching hostility toward censorship." She acknowledged that the "strangely stubborn Mr. Frohnmayer" refused to drop the language, contrary to the recommendations of the National Council and the independent commission. Then a federal judge (surprise!) found it unconstitutional. She concluded, "The [loyalty] pledge is history. The agency's luster has been dimmed — but not half so much as Mr. Frohnmayer's credibility."

So I called up Mary Cantwell. I told her the "mild but tricky" law had clearly been unconstitutional. I had known it, and the only way to get rid of it had been for a court to say so. It was everybody's problem; I had had to shine a light on it. She was unimpressed. The *New York Times* had taken a profound interest in litigation on this issue brought against us by the New School, and apparently the settlement of that suit on the same terms as the *Lewitzky* decision had precipitated the editorial. Cantwell thought what I had to say was "very interesting." That was the end of it.

I thought that perhaps members of the National Council would come to my defense, but there was silence. So my staff called a few of them in New York to ask if they might be willing to write a letter to the editor. Harvey Lichtenstein wrote one, a lukewarm endorsement based on a draft we had written for him. I called John Brademas, who had been cochairman of the independent commission. He was not sympathetic either. He thought that the court challenge was some-thing I hadn't needed to provoke. Okay, I did it because I thought it was right, not to be popular. But I still hoped that somewhere, some-one would understand what I was doing.

I launched a campaign to prop up my image. In *Presbyterian Church USA* magazine, I explained that while the public isn't entitled to a plebiscite on every piece of art funded by the NEA, we had an obligation to be exceptionally thorough in our process because we were using taxpayers' money. As for those religious leaders who attacked the Endowment, I noted that religion and art have much in common. Both seek human fulfillment and expression and try to make sense of a world that is chaotic and confusing. Both try to help people live in ways that are beneficial to themselves and their companions. Much of the world's great art has been prompted by religion, and many people — J. S. Bach, for example — have melded art and religion to the glory of both.

Then I wrote a piece for the *Washington Post* entitled "It's Your Sixty-Eight Cents so Let's Talk about It." That sum is what each citizen pays in taxes, on average, for everything the National Endowment for the Arts does. "The Endowment," I said, "has helped bring 70 new choruses and 120 new symphony orchestras into being in the last twenty-five years. . . . It has helped pay for 364 new theaters at which you have seen plays, both good and bad, depicting love and hate and joy and envy and success and failure — just like our lives." I described how the panels work, how the National Council reviews the panels' recommendations, and how the staff of the Endowment is dedicated to assuring that good art is funded. Concerning the controversial grants, I said that while the Endowment is for everybody, not everything it does is for everyone. Some of our tax dollars support bridges or roads we will never drive over. We might not agree with the agricultural, health, or labor policies of the country, but our taxes still support them. It's part of the social contract. Some controversies we resolve and some stay with us, but we resolve few by ignoring them. Sometimes art provides a vehicle, a forum, for that public debate. A play like *Driving Miss Daisy* prods our conscience gently. Other works prod debate more confrontationally.

This opinion piece, which was widely reprinted, did do some good — not so much for my image, but by putting into perspective what the Endowment is and does. At the same time, we began working on a short video that would depict the Endowment's work visually, since much of what we funded simply could not be described adequately in words.

I went out to visit the troops in Alabama, Mississippi, West Virginia, Pennsylvania, and Kansas. (By now I had been to more than half the states, and I intended to visit them all.) I saw the magnificent Shakespeare Theater in Montgomery, built and donated by the industrialist and arts patron Red Blount. The theater's company had originally been in the town of Anniston, but it had suffered from financial difficulties. Blount said that he would build it a theater, but the company would have to go to Montgomery. With the battle cry "Better Red than Dead," it moved and flourished.

I attended a reception in Columbus, Mississippi, thirty miles south of Tupelo, where the Reverend Donald Wildmon hangs out. Tupelo has a vigorous cultural life, and being associated with Wildmon is for some of its citizens a profound embarrassment. At the reception people kept coming by and stuffing letters and notes into my suit pockets, urging me not to write off Mississippi just because of Wildmon. To the contrary, I found Mississippi full of culture, both folk and classical, and wholly delightful.

We decided to see all of Kansas in one day. Starting from Kansas City, we drove to Lawrence for a gallery reception where we met local leaders, and from there to Topeka, where we had lunch and I gave a short speech. Then we flew in a small plane to Russell, Hayes, and Salina. I have seldom seen as many new and glorious performing arts facilities as I saw in Kansas. I learned that every federal arts dollar spent in Kansas generates seventeen additional dollars to make these projects happen. The state enjoys a total of $18 million in arts activity, and one in ten of its citizens volunteers in some artistic endeavor.

Flying back to Kansas City, we followed an electrical storm. I asked the pilot how the radar worked and he explained that green meant there were no clouds, brown meant clouds, and red meant heavy clouds. I watched with dismay as the screen turned brown, then more red, then completely red. Lightning was flashing all around us, and as we came into Kansas City the pilot turned off the radar — he just couldn't stand bad news. A few hours later, grateful not to have been planted in a Kansas cornfield, I took my dusted-off image back to Washington.

Soon after I returned from a visit with "real people," royalty bestowed a visit on the United States, when Monaco's Prince Rainier showed up with his son for the opening of the Metropolitan Opera. The prince set the record for falling asleep in public. Sitting next to Barbara Bush at the beginning of *La Bohème*, he was snoring gently, his head near her shoulder, in fifteen minutes flat. To prove this was no fluke, he bettered his record, twelve minutes, at the start of the second act.

My nomination for American royalty, Wallace Stegner, was more than awake when he came to tea at my office to accept the Endowment's award for a distinguished career in literature. He admitted that he had had some doubts about whether he should accept the award, but after talking with me, he said he was glad that he had and he hoped this award would help get one more book out of him.

Meanwhile, the media consultants who had volunteered to help us insisted that it was critical for me to be profiled in the *New York Times*. Such a profile could turn around my image, they insisted, and they could set it up. When David Johnston of the *Times* came in to do the interview, he led off by saying that he didn't know much about the Endowment and hadn't followed the controversy. I should have stopped the interview there, but I didn't. The story that appeared on May 3 began, "The cliché around town on [Frohnmayer] is that he arrived in the capital without a grasp of the art of politics or the politics of art, and not much has changed in the eighteen months he has been here." I was one of the Bush administration's "most polarizing and least nimble figures." Johnston had contacted all of the usual sources who could be counted on to give negative comments, including Charlotte Murphy, of the National Association of Artists' Organizations, who said of my defense of artists, "It was too little, too late," and a National Council member who damned me with faint praise, saying, "He's learned a lot since [Artists Space]."

There were two lessons here. One was to listen to my wife more often — she had counseled against the interview. The other was that I was going to get trashed but I didn't need to invite it. The article did help me recognize that not much I consciously tried to do would help my image. What I had to remember — and this was a lesson I had to relearn about every six months — was that the only assessment of my performance that ultimately mattered was my own.

A controversial film we had funded also helped me remember this lesson. I was in Pittsburgh in late March 1991, talking to arts groups, when news stories began to break about *Poison*. Perhaps I had heard about the film before, but it hadn't registered. Just like the airplane radar that kept getting darker as we flew over Kansas, my office called throughout the day with increasing concern about what looked like the next crisis. I was at my host's house for dinner, along with twenty other people, when the office called again. While I was speaking with them, my host, ever attentive, took one look at my face and slapped an adult beverage into my hand. I excused myself from the dinner party and caught the first plane back to Washington.

The problem was my old nemesis, Donald Wildmon, who had taken up *Poison* as his latest crusade. Wildmon thought the film was called *Homo,* which was not surprising, because he hadn't seen it, but that hadn't stopped him from bombarding Congress with a letter branding it a "porno film."

I decided to see for myself (several of my staff members had already seen it). As soon as I got back to Washington I watched it on the VCR in my office, dreading each new scene in case my worst expectations would be realized. They never were. When the film was over, I looked at Anne Radice (this occurred during her first week on the job as senior deputy), and we both shrugged. What was the big deal?

The film, 120 minutes long, was composed of three different stories, intermixed and shot in three classic movie styles: documentary, thirties horror film, and fifties gangster film. The first story, "Hero," was about a young boy who was abused and neglected and witnessed domestic violence that eventually led to the destruction of his family. The second story, "Horror," featured a medical scientist who accidentally drank a concoction that gave him a contagious, disfiguring disease. It was a loose allegory of the AIDS epidemic. The third story, "Homo," was set in a French prison and dealt with brutal prison conditions, including rape.

The entire film cost $250,000, of which $25,000 had come from the Endowment during my tenure, to help defray postproduction costs. Although it was not a film for all audiences, it was artistic and serious, dealing with difficult issues. *Newsweek*'s reviewer, responding to both the film and the trouble Wildmon had stirred up, said, "It's precisely the kind of imaginative, form-stretching and increasingly endangered species of filmmaking the NEA ought to be supporting. . . . *Poison* doesn't go down easy, and it isn't meant to. But we should thank the NEA, not curse them, for helping it on its way." Moreover, the film had won the grand prize at the Sundance Film Festival and had been recommended to the Arts Endowment by a panel composed of experts with impeccable film credentials, including an Oscar winner.

As we had so many times before, my staff — Randy McAusland, Cindy Rand, Julie Davis, Rose DiNapoli, and Jason Hall, who was acting public affairs director while Jack Lichtenstein was off in the Persian Gulf with his army reserve unit — and I sat around the big table in my office. This was the inaugural crisis for Jason, as well as for Anne Radice and Margaret Wyszomirski. Predictably, those who hadn't done this drill before counseled caution: distance the NEA from the film, disclaim it. The others argued that the film itself was the best response. It was not obscene or pornographic by any stretch of the imagination. This film gave us an opportunity to demonstrate the slander that had been visited on the Endowment over so many projects for so long. Our response should be bold. If we let this issue get rolling, as we had before, we would never get the facts before the public.

I called a news conference for Friday, March 29, taking care to invite not just the media regulars but the fundamentalist press and the organizations that had been so vocal in their criticism of us. The room was full. I had been advised by my staff and some public relations experts I consulted first to establish myself — to let the audience know who John Frohnmayer was. I said that I had grown up in a small southern Oregon town, played football, sung in the church choir, been loved by my family, and learned what I believed were American values: honesty, love and respect, integrity, reason and love

applications would not violate the First Amendment." Knowing that I disagreed, he said that the legal basis on which agency actions should be defended in litigation was a decision "that must be made by the Justice Department."

I responded,

> I am writing you personally to assure that you understand that the litigation strategy proposed by your office is contrary to the best interests of this agency. . . . While we as lawyers can argue about the correct legal analysis of these issues, I, as Chairman of the National Endowment for the Arts, must advance the long-term interests of the Endowment. [The arguments advanced in your letter] are contrary to every public statement I have made on behalf of the Endowment and I will not allow them to be cast as our position and, if interrogated, would disavow them.

(The Justice Department also wanted to advance the position that nothing in the Endowment's authorizing legislation prohibited us from making decisions on the basis of preferred content as opposed to artistic quality.)

On July 1, Gerson wrote back, repeating the argument that the First Amendment does not prohibit the government from denying grants because of objections to the viewpoints expressed. But even *Rust* did not go that far; it said, "This court has recognized that the existence of a 'Government subsidy' . . . does not justify the restriction of speech in areas that have 'been traditionally open to the public for expressive activity.' " Nonetheless, Gerson suggested that since the administration's position was what he had described, that would "seem to circumscribe the options available." In other words, I wouldn't be allowed to disavow it. Since he agreed that we could not solve this problem, he was forwarding our correspondence to the executive branch for its decision.

A week later, C. Boyden Gray, the president's lawyer, called to inform me that he wanted to let the Justice Department make the strongest argument it could make. He personally didn't like the abortion decision, but ours was a case where he thought the Justice Department ought to do the lawyering. I responded that the issue had far greater significance for the administration than just whether our case was won or lost. If the Justice Department made its argument, the administration would be billed as doing what Congress refused to do, namely, imposing content restrictions on the Arts Endowment. I said again that such a position would be contrary to every public statement I had made and, not incidentally, to the position of the president, whose proposed legislation on the Endowment the year before had said, "After much careful thought and discussion, it is our conclusion that the legislation proposed here, which contains no content restrictions . . . will best serve the American public." I argued and I argued, and finally, to get me off the phone, Gray agreed to set up a meeting with Gerson and me.

I asked him not to invite anyone else. I didn't want to be shouted down by a bevy of Justice Department lawyers, and anyway, from my point of view, the decision was one more of policy than of law.

On the day of the meeting, July 30, Leslie H. Southwick, Gerson's assistant, testified to the Senate that the enabling legislation of the Endowment and *Rust* v. *Sullivan* would surely permit the NEA to decline to fund racist propaganda even if it was "artistically presented." "The First Amendment does not require Congress to write blank checks," he said. As I read the First Amendment, it exists precisely to protect minorities against the power of the government. And while Southwick and Gerson might frame their argument skillfully, they were after the suppression of dangerous ideas.

C. Boyden Gray's office in the White House was dark and filled with stacks of papers. We sat around his conference table and Gerson made his pitch, which was now slightly different. A successful motion for summary judgment would avoid depositions and document discovery and prevent a flood of similarly directed lawsuits. The summary judgment argument is a loser, I replied. The Justice Department's brief does not even mention the controlling case, which was decided by the same judge who will decide this one. No matter how carefully crafted, this argument will reflect poorly on the White House and everything the Arts Endowment stands for.

Gray wondered why we couldn't simply argue that because the chairman's decisions are subjective, a court cannot review them. I said that I didn't believe a summary judgment motion was necessary at all, but if one was to be made, that line of argument was preferable to me.

Gray sent us back to try a new draft. Gerson didn't say much after the meeting and apparently didn't want to continue the battle. I was astounded by my success. I had been certain that after politely listening, Gray would direct Justice to make its arguments and me to be quiet. Ultimately, the brief was filed with only two incidental references to *Rust* and no argument that content-based decisions were legal.

During the summer of 1991, for a change, the controversies were not ours — at least, not all of them. Take, for example, the nomination by the White House of Carol Iannone to the National Council for the Humanities. Her credentials were slender but her conservative ideology clear. The nomination was held up in the Senate for six months and then again postponed, this time at the request of Lynne Cheney, who commenced a blitz on Capitol Hill, enlisting the aid of Vice President Quayle and taking Iannone from office to office herself. Ted Kennedy told the Democratic troops that he needed to win this one, and the vote to reject was substantially along party lines.

Then came the recriminations: Iannone had been the subject of a political litmus test and was rejected because she was conservative and outspoken. What in the world could the White House have expected? Carol Iannone's qualifications would have taken her to the top no more than Clarence Thomas's would have. The White House could not deny with a straight face that it was nominating on the basis of political ideology rather than professional qualifications. Why then the insult when Congress rejected the nominee on the same basis?

The problem, of course, was that both sides were wrong. Ideally, the White House would nominate the best-qualified candidate. Congress would review the qualifications and, finding them in order, extend the traditional courtesy to the executive branch by approving the nomination without delay. The trouble was indicative of the malaise that had overcome government. Each side was playing politics as if politics itself were the end, not governing and serving the American people.

The next two skirmishes belonged to Betsy Broun at the National Museum of American Art, a part of the Smithsonian. In mid-July, an exhibition entitled "Eadweard Meybridge and Contemporary American Photography" took on a different focus when Broun removed a piece by the photographer Sol LeWitt, claiming it was humiliating to women. The LeWitt work, which consisted of a series of peepholes through which one observed an advancing image of a nude woman, was offensive to Broun because she thought it focused on the woman's pubic area. The immediate and well-orchestrated outrage of the show's original curator and its contributing artists followed, and after a good deal of bullying (a technique being honed to perfection in the art world), Broun restored the piece to the show.

Almost simultaneously, Senator Ted Stevens took issue with another show at the same museum, "The West as America: Reinterpreting Images of the Frontier, 1820–1920." Stevens accused the Smithsonian of having a left-leaning agenda. "We from the West who live here in the East are really under attack all the time," he claimed. "To see that exhibit . . . really sets me off. Why should people come to your institution and see history that's so perverted?"

Granted, subtlety was not the exhibition's strong suit. To conclude that the artist who depicted cowboys defending a water hole while Indians attacked was commenting on the oppression of minorities by the white expansionists is not a conclusion all viewers would rush to embrace. Nonetheless, Stevens's heavy-handed attack, and his parallel criticism of a television series on Christopher Columbus that presented the views of the celebrated Mexican writer Carlos Fuentes ("a Marxist noncitizen"), bore a certain resemblance to the performances we had come to expect from Jesse Helms. Some suggested that what had really set Stevens off was a documentary entitled *Black Tide*, which was not financially supported by the Smithsonian but was shown at one of its museums. Stevens, Alaska's senior senator, claimed that the film, which dealt with the *Exxon Valdez* oil spill, was "not balanced." Another rumor was that a Smithsonian employee had referred to Senator Stevens as "brain-dead" and the comment had floated back to him.

We shared the biggest flap of the summer with PBS over the airing of Marlon Riggs's film *Tongues Untied,* a documentary about homosexual black men. The title refers to their speaking out about homophobia, their sexuality, and their role in society. The filmmaker received a $5,000 grant from the NEA in 1988 to help make the film, and *P.O.V. (Point of View)* on PBS received a $250,000 grant for its 1991 programming, in which *Tongues Untied* was one show of many. The film had won the top prize at the Berlin International Film Festival, a blue ribbon at the American Film and Video Festival, and a Special Jury Award at the USA Film Festival. The *P.O.V.* series had posted two Academy Awards, three Emmys, three Peabody Awards, and a host of others over the years. Nonetheless, Donald Wildmon entered stage right with another letter assault on Congress, urging, on the one hand, that stations not show the film, and on the other, that members of Congress watch it. They would experience firsthand, he said, the kind of blasphemy and promotion of the homosexual lifestyle of which the Endowment was guilty.

Many PBS stations (at least eighteen in the fifty largest television markets) declined to show the film. Many that did show it did so at 11:00 P.M. or 3:00 A.M. While Wildmon deemed the film erotic and offensive, the eroticism consisted mainly of males kissing, and it was clear that Wildmon's attack was against homosexuals generally. In an earlier letter to Congress, this one complaining about the San Francisco Gay and Lesbian Film Festival, Wildmon had been so overtly homophobic that I had responded to Congress, "Mr. Wildmon's complaint, stripped of rhetoric, seems to be that he doesn't believe federal funds should go to homosexuals. The Endowment does not blacklist nor does it give or refuse grants on the basis of sexual orientation."

Tongues Untied showed black men rapping, street talking, and dancing. The language was not unlike what I heard every morning and evening on the subway. It was reminiscent of what Judge John Woolsey had described in his famous opinion on James Joyce's novel *Ulysses* in 1933: "The words which are criticized as dirty are old Saxon words known to almost all men and, I venture, to many women, and would be naturally and habitually used, I believe, by the types of folk whose life, physical and mental, Joyce is seeking to describe." Marlon Riggs put the issue slightly differently: "A society that shuts its eyes cannot grow or change or discover what's really decent in the world."

P.O.V.'s mission was just what its name suggests: it was a forum in which independent filmmakers could express their points of view to challenge or expand the thinking of the show's viewers. Unfortunately, what one brought to the viewing (or nonviewing) of *Tongues Untied* probably determined whether one thought it was homosexual trash or an artistic window into the lives of a group of Americans. But our inability or unwillingness to deal with differences was a persuasive reason to air the film, not to reject it. In spite of that, we were in a summer of intimidation, and finally 174 public broadcasting stations refused to show *Tongues Untied.*

Every few months, James J. Kilpatrick would blast the NEA in his syndicated column. At a reception late one evening I was introduced to him.

"I've been knocking the hell out of you," he said.

"It would be more meaningful if you knew what you were talking about," I replied. "Why don't you come in, and I'll show you what it is we fund and how we do it."

"Maybe I'll do that," he said.

He did come for a visit. When I greeted him, I said, "Always glad to meet the enemy." He demurred, muttering something about his wife's being on the board of an art museum. Jack Lichtenstein and I spoke with him for an hour while he took a few notes on the back of an envelope. He requested manuscripts from some poetry grantees, saying that he was competent to judge the quality of literature. We were glad to comply. Off he went with a stack of papers (he also made a Freedom of Information Act request and obtained more materials).

As the months passed, I wondered whether we would hear from him again. At last he wrote about the poets, saying, "It pains me to say this, for my reputation is at stake, but the poems, on the whole, were damnedly good . . . their imagery was fine . . . their free verse carried a wallop." And then, as if being complimentary offended his basic nature, he launched an attack on *Tongues Untied.* According to Howard Rosenberg of the *Los Angeles Times,* Kilpatrick had not seen the picture. Nonetheless, he found it grossly offensive and urged me to stiffen my spine. Thanks, Jack. Who knows what he would have said if he had bothered to watch the film?

Burnout, or the perfectly understandable desire to return to a normal life, was taking its toll on the NEA staff. By midsummer, Julie Davis had returned to law practice in Portland, Jack Lichtenstein, back from the Gulf war, was going into the public relations business for himself, Cindy Rand had taken a promotion to the Department of Transportation, and Rose DiNapoli had taken a staff position with the Committee on Education and Labor in the House of Representatives. Staff meetings weren't fun anymore. Those battle-scarred veterans with whom I could laugh, at least sometimes, were replaced by political appointees such as Bobbi Dunn, who took Rose's place as congressional liaison, and Anne Radice.

After a staff retreat in the spring of 1991, Radice told me that she had never seen an agency in which issues were so freely discussed among the employees; she was enthusiastic about the openness. She got over that quickly, and after the first few disagreements simply sat stern-faced, crossed-armed, and mute at our meetings. I tried to draw her out. She would say, "You know how I feel about this stuff." I would ask her to articulate her position, and the most she ever said was that it was important for us not to offend Congress. She cautioned me repeatedly about the California congresswoman Barbara Boxer and Congressman Sidney Yates. "They're Democrats," she would say. "You can't trust them, because you are a Republican."

Moreover, I was beginning to suspect that the information I was receiving from Bobbi Dunn, particularly about the positions of members of Congress, was being filtered. I knew she was a conservative when the White House endorsed her, but because she came highly recommended, I welcomed her, for two reasons: first, we needed help with the conservatives on the Hill, and second, she could start right away. But when she told me that Senator Leahy thought the Endowment should be looking at considerations other than artistic excellence in making its judgments, it just didn't ring true. Whom did she hear this from? I asked. Ellen Lovell, Leahy's chief of staff, she said. I knew Ellen — had known her for a dozen years, since she was a former state arts agency director. When I called her, she was horrified. What she had expressed was sympathy for my difficult tightrope act. Of course artistic excellence was still the key, and there was no feeling on Senator Leahy's part that difficult categories should be scrapped.

After that, Bobbi was reluctant to disclose her sources to me. She said staff members wouldn't confide in her if they knew it might get back to their bosses. Similarly, since Anne Radice was the liaison with the White House, I got only the information she decided I should hear. Except for my direct contacts with the Hill and the White House, I was becoming increasingly isolated.

EIGHTEEN

OUR ANNUAL APPROPRIATIONS bill passed the House in the summer of 1991 with little difficulty. Congressman Crane again proposed his amendment to abolish the Endowment. This year it was defeated 435–65, by one more vote than the year before. That was reassuring. Congressman Cliff Stearns, a Florida Republican, proposed to slap our hand with a budget reduction for funding the film *Poison.* That amendment was defeated by only thirty votes, but as I watched on C-Span, the number of votes against Stearns's amendment continued to decrease after the time for voting had ended. Congressmen can change their votes after the result is clear, and while a statement to that effect appears in the *Congressional Record,* the practice is a lily-livered enterprise befitting the crassly political.

As summer melded with fall, however, a pall of ugliness swept over Congress, exemplified both by the confirmation hearings of Clarence Thomas for the Supreme Court and by a renewed assault on the National Endowment for the Arts. As politics got meaner, principles fled to the shadows, and the display on Capitol Hill was, in a word, depressing.

The first salvo came from Senator Nancy Kassebaum, who in early September declared herself to "care deeply about the arts community" before proposing a $17.4 million cut in our budget — a 13 percent reduction. I had talked to her the day before and she had explained that she was troubled about some grants that had been awarded. Which ones? I asked. She was vague. "There is no way I

think and to reflect on an incredibly brutal act in an allegedly civilized society.

Some weeks later I received a letter from the managing editor of *the portable lower east side,* acknowledging that I had defended the poem. "I don't believe that a thank you would be appropriate," he said, "because what you did was a matter of personal principles and a person shouldn't be thanked for his principles. I simply want to state that I greatly admire your action, and can only hope that someday should I find myself in a similar situation I might respond as well as you did." But members of the White House staff were not interested in the poem's meaning. Buchanan hadn't picked it up yet, but Skinner was sure he would. They were looking for the usual political solution, which was to assuage whatever conservative group screamed loudest about their individual and collective outrage. Constance Horner, who replaced Chase Untermeyer as the head of Presidential Personnel after he left to run the Voice of America, received an earful on a satellite television program hosted by the conservative leader Paul Weyrich. Allegedly, she set about besieging Skinner to engineer my rapid departure.

I have never met Constance Horner and could not pick her out of a crowd. But during this time I did have a sobering series of phone conversations with her. I had been trying since June 1991 to replace Selina Ottum. After being told that several candidates I preferred for the position of deputy for partnerships would not pass political muster, I settled on Burton Woolf, a highly experienced administrator who had been out of the field for several years and therefore, I hoped, carried little political baggage. Presidential Personnel sat on my request for four months. Finally I called Horner and asked pointblank whether she was going to approve Burt Woolf.

"I can't agree with that recommendation," she said. "We want someone who has stronger allegiance to the Republican party."

"Were you ever going to tell me that?" I asked.

"I heard you are leaving. It's all around town."

"I have no immediate plans to leave," I said. "I'm talking about Burt Woolf. He is clearly qualified to handle this job."

"It has to be someone who has strong political commitments to the president or the party," she said.

"Burt Woolf has strong backing from respected Republicans," I replied. "What more do you need?"

"We have to have someone who espouses the Reagan-Bush philosophy," she said.

"Reagan and Bush differ on many issues, including the arts," I said. "Does the president know you are looking for Reagan people?"

There was a pause; then, "I just need good evidence that this is someone who would support the president no matter what."

There it was, without apology: loyalty mattered more than ability. I wasn't going to get anyone, that was clear. Nor was I going to get control of my own congressional liaison office or public affairs office, no matter what kind of directives I issued. Some Endowment employees were telling me that there were in effect two chairpersons with differing agendas, Anne and myself. The political appointees knew I couldn't fire them.

Anne could not have been more curious about whether I might voluntarily resign. For example, after I had lunch with Randy one day, she pumped him about whether I had given any clues. The accumulation of controversies and the progression of the primaries were thunderheads building for an afternoon storm. It was no surprise, then, when Beth Stoner came running down the hall after me as I was walking to the elevator one day and, with a face drained of color, said that Sam Skinner wanted to see me right away.

I felt a little jump in my stomach. I wasn't looking forward to getting fired, but the longer I stayed, the more certain it was. I asked Beth to reply that I couldn't see Skinner that day but to set the appointment as soon as his schedule permitted. I wanted some time to think out what I would say.

The next day, I told my friend Mark Edleman during lunch that I had a 1:30 appointment with Skinner and was probably going to be fired. He couldn't believe it, and said it wouldn't happen. As I walked up the White House drive from the Pennsylvania Avenue guardhouse, I hoped that Mark was right, that Skinner wanted to talk to me about something else. Since I had declared my intent to leave, the job had become precious — the autumn of a lifelong quest to enhance the arts. A few more months could make a big difference.

So on February 20, 1992, Sam Skinner canned me in front of the fire in Sununu's old office. The "resignation" was front-page news in the major papers. The press was generous, as always:

> Mr. Frohnmayer was a victim of his own management style.

> Frohnmayer had two problems: he took on an impossible job and he performed it ineptly.

> Rarely has a federal agency head waffled like the NEA chairman did.

Congressman Armey, who claimed to have brought "Wild Thing" to the White House's attention after he received his letter from Wildmon, said he was "pleased if in any way I helped bring [the firing] about." Pat Buchanan, in his ongoing presidential quest, claimed his first scalp, and Donald Wildmon's newsletter chortled that his efforts in opposing the NEA had paid off.

After I had announced my resignation and delivered an emotional farewell to my staff — I even hugged Bobbi Dunn, whom I can't stand — Leah and I decided that it would be healthy for me to spend the weekend in the country by myself. As I walked through the woods in the beautiful foothills of the Blue Ridge Mountains of northern Virginia, I felt once again as if a huge burden had been lifted. It was not just the relief of no longer having to speak for an administration with which I had almost nothing in common, but a welcome realization that I would soon be a private person again, able to think, speak, and act on my own convictions. I grieved, not for my departure but for the Endowment and its future direction.

During the weekend I built a chair, or at least I tried. I liked those nifty rustic bentwood chairs, so I collected branches and vines and went to work with my saw and my drill and some dowels. When I finished, the chair looked slightly askew, like something out of Van

Gogh's bedroom. When I tried sitting on it, it exploded apart — perhaps an appropriate metaphor for my Endowment days.

Within hours of my announcement that I was leaving, the reign of terror started at the Endowment. The first missive was a memorandum from Anne Radice on February 26, saying that Presidential Personnel had called to inform her that all personnel actions were frozen until an acting chairman was appointed. No one could be hired or fired. "They will let me know when the freeze is lifted," she said. "I will inform the personnel committee and the personnel department."

I called Anne into my office and asked her what she thought she was doing.

"Well, Jan Naylor called me and said, you know, that when somebody resigns, all personnel actions are frozen."

"Under what authority?"

"I don't know, I'll ask her. I was surprised. I understand that when somebody leaves, you want to protect people who are already here and you don't want people to feel that they are in danger of being shifted around or sent to Siberia."

I said that I wanted to protect those who might be subject to retribution for having worked for me. "I hope this doesn't get nasty with the White House," I said, "because I'm trying very hard to hold my peace, and the message ought to be conveyed to them that if they start throwing spitballs over here, I won't hesitate to be tough — and I think you know I can be as tough as anybody."

"I know that," said Anne.

"Jan Naylor should communicate directly with me on this issue. So I'll expect a call. I just think, Anne, it's terribly important for this to be a smooth transition, and I will help you in every way I can until it becomes impossible for me to do so. So please make that message clear to them."

Anne said that she appreciated my offer of help and she too hoped for a smooth transition. After meeting with Naylor, she wrote me a memo saying that the personnel freeze was routine. Naylor didn't give me the courtesy of a call, and in my view the federal regulations that Presidential Personnel cited did not authorize this action.

Upon the changing of the guard, the sycophants lined up at Anne's door — not just those who had been a part of the cabal (the politicals), but Steve Klink, from personnel; Brian O'Doherty, from the media department; and others who were survivors in this very political town. No announcement designating Radice as the successor-apparent had been made, but she was obviously the one with White House connections (through Jan Naylor), and survivors have an unerring nose for where the power has gone.

I began to turn over the problems to Anne, and there were dozens of them every day. As far as I was concerned, she should make the decisions she would have to defend. Although I had asked to stay until May 1 and Sam Skinner had specifically cleared that date with the president, I now had mixed feelings about it. On the one hand, I hoped that I could accomplish a few more things — the education conference and the rural arts conference, to name two — but on the other hand, the atmosphere was becoming polluted. Jane Smith was talking to Michael McLaughlin, from Randy McAusland's office, in the hall one day when one of the political appointees came around the corner. Michael abruptly walked away in mid-sentence. He later called Jane and apologized, saying, "I have to keep my job." Jane, of course, being from the general counsel's office, was closely identified with me, and I was now poison.

Anne approached E'Vonne one day in early April and said, "There is no reason for John to be in the building. I'll give you whatever job you want if you can get him to leave." E'Vonne just smiled sweetly and said, "When I leave, it will be with my integrity intact. Talk to him yourself."

Some lessons from my experience with the Endowment were coming into focus. Always when I talked about procedure, my audience's eyes glazed over. Yet procedure is the linchpin that keeps political whim and individual caprice from destroying the NEA's process and credibility. The Endowment has two gifts to give, money and the acknowledgment of excellence. Political favors and any other aberration that bypasses procedure dull the acknowledgment of excellence and cheapen the Endowment.

When everyone else was hurling political bombs, Frohnmayer was talking about procedure. It infuriated and frustrated many of my supporters. Yes, the nimble are admired in Washington; as Everett Dirksen once said, "I am a man of principle, and one of my principles is flexibility." But being politically savvy is no virtue if all it means is that one does no more than manipulate the process. I understand the process in Washington, but I do not embrace it. America deserves better, and we will get it only when citizens demand better. Compromise is indeed the art of politics, but principles, clear procedure, and articulated goals are the stuff of a successful administration.

In the case of the arts, outrage had replaced analysis. People such as Wildmon and Buchanan were easily outraged, often by art they hadn't seen, as described by those who probably hadn't seen it either. When confronted with his ignorance about the artworks he was denouncing, Wildmon said, "You don't have to be in the sewer to know it smells." People were so quick to take offense in part because it was easy. Rage doesn't require thought; it's pure emotion. It is an immature response, manipulative and selfish.

Because some art is on the margin, pushing the boundaries of our thought and our tolerance, and because some conservatism is rigid and uncompromising, we will always have clashes. After two and a half years of art wars in which I personally took plenty of hits, I believe unequivocally that such controversy is healthy. But a degree of social goodwill, generosity of spirit, call it what you will, is necessary for communication. That is in short supply, and we won't get it back by governmental decree. We will get it back person by person — through individual resolve to listen and try to understand.

The arts can never make their case alone. When the Endowment was reauthorized in 1990, it was with the support of a noble coalition of labor, mayors, the American Bar Association, humanists, teachers, librarians, chambers of commerce, and dozens of other segments of the American public who recognized that the arts are an integral part of what defines society. This was in many ways an unnatural coalition, and keeping it together after the immediate crisis passed was not possible. But it did represent some of the elements of our society who will have to hammer out the new clauses in our nation's social contract.

Members of Congress who received hate mail about the NEA were seldom willing to write back saying, "You are misinformed" and explaining that the Endowment either didn't fund what it was accused of funding or that the story the critics had been told was at best partial and at worst probably false — much less that hearing (and even supporting with tax dollars) opinions with which we disagree is a reward, not a burden, of democracy. The rules of honorable engagement in political warfare — that is, truthful claims, reliance on facts, and a recognition that ultimately, regardless of political affiliation, the common good is our goal — have vanished and will not return again until enough of the populace demands them (or a daring politician gets some publicity for reinventing them). Congress, I fear, reflects the disengagement of the ordinary citizen. While Congress has earned the low regard in which it is held, those very citizens (ourselves) who allow its members to preen and bluster instead of honestly addressing problems are to blame.

For me, the important questions that came out of the art wars were the ones that applied to life generally: How can I do better next time — what did I learn? Can I anticipate the next crisis and be better prepared? What sources of energy and renewal can I use to continue to participate? And most important, perhaps, to what extent have I been true to myself, to that which I believe? For me, that meant asking how I changed through the Endowment experience, and why. That was the question I confronted on the weekend of March 21.

Several weeks after the announcement of my departure, Joe Duffy, the president of American University and a past chairman of the National Endowment for the Humanities, called and asked if I would be part of a freedom-of-expression seminar sponsored by American University and the National Press Club for foreign journalists, mostly from Third World countries. My role would be to speak on the First Amendment, particularly its exportability to other lands. The topic fascinated me, because I knew that our struggles in the United States were tame compared to what many of these journalists had been through: seeing loved ones murdered, being chained to their beds or imprisoned without charge or trial.

I agreed to speak, without giving much thought to what I would say. During subsequent conversations with Sandy Ungar, the head of American University's School of Communications, and Scott Armstrong, the coordinator of the conference, I settled on a time (March 23) and topic, making the caveat that I would talk only about the First Amendment. I had already had preliminary discussions with the press club about giving a speech in early May, after I had left the Endowment, about my own experience with governmental intrusions into the speech and ideas of artists.

The next week Kathy Christie called from my public affairs office to say that I was being billed as the press club's featured speaker on March 23 and my topic was to be the NEA — a tell-all. I was horrified. I called Scott and said I wouldn't do it. He in turn called the National Press Club, which said that if I canceled, I would not be invited to speak there again. Besides, the club had an immutable policy that no one spoke twice during a calendar year, so it was now or not at all. Scott assured me that American University would provide another forum in May and apologized for the screwup, and I set out to write the First Amendment speech. But I couldn't.

On Saturday morning, March 21, I was working with a draft that my steadfast assistant Keith Donohue had prepared. Nothing seemed worth saying. The parameters were too narrowly drawn. To continue the silence I had been keeping since being told to announce my resignation was, in front of foreign journalists who had sacrificed so much, both foolish and small. I had no future in this Republican administration. Indeed, as the word *Republican* was being defined by those who seemed to be in control of the party, I wasn't one at all. The political code of *omertà* applied, it seemed to me, to those who wanted another government job, and I did not. Sometime between 9:00 A.M. on Saturday and 11:00 A.M. on Sunday, I realized that I had changed. No longer was I a detached observer of society. Still an imperfect citizen, I could not tend my own garden or be silent (and comfortable) in the face of increasing evidence that our society was jettisoning what few ideals it had left.

So I wrote my National Press Club speech — about the history of censorship, the impediments to having a vital First Amendment, and the political cowardice of those who attack art as a way of sending messages of hate, exclusion, and prejudice. It is up to our generation, I said, as it was to all who have gone before us, to reaffirm the First Amendment protection of and from religion, of free association, of speech, of press, and of thought. We are impeded by anti-intellectualism (the failure to put our faith in rational discourse to solve our problems), by the tension between our protection from a state religion and the suggestion that we as a country are chosen by God, and by the electronic isolation that television gives us, so that we don't assemble and argue out our problems anymore.

Once again I asserted that art is part of the answer to rekindling our free spirit. The arts foster creativity, build community, and teach children to learn. They support our economic successes as well. The answer to the debate about the Endowment, I said, is not to concentrate on what is "decent" or what offends certain people. The First Amendment protects the speaker, particularly the speaker of difficult or unpopular ideas. Congress shouldn't need cover so its members can claim that they voted against obscenity; it should fear the sound bite that says, "My opponent jettisoned our precious right of free expression to cover his fanny." The Arts Endowment would be saved not by restrictive policies but by letting all voices be heard.

The reaction to the speech was astonishing. Requests for copies poured in to the Endowment. (The press office, now firmly under the control of the politicals, refused to provide them.) The speech continued to be rerun on C-Span stations across the nation for weeks afterward. But what was so surprising to me was that this message, so fundamental and simple, was to so many people exciting and new. It was proof of how far we have drifted, as a nation, from our philosophical roots.

And so the National Press Club speech was really a reaffirmation. Throughout my ordeal at the Endowment, I had been concerned that my boys, Jason and Aaron, seeing at close quarters the difficulties of a political job, would forever forswear public service. But in the end, this job was liberating. It reminded me of what I believe, and that those beliefs can sometimes change. It reminded me that for every schmuck in public office — and there are plenty of them — there are good, honest, and dedicated people as well. It reminded me that our societal drift can be cured only by personal involvement. And it demonstrated renewal.

When Mount St. Helens exploded in 1980, it laid waste to everything in the path of its six-hundred-degree gases, leaving a gray and despoiled landscape in which landmarks had been erased, trees laid down like so many toothpicks — an aspect so dismal that it seemed it would never recover. Not a fir bough, a blade of grass, or a spray of lupine survived. Yet marvelously, the next spring, green began to reappear, pushing up through yards of gray ash, emerging seemingly from nowhere. And so it is with both the artist and the human spirit that the artist describes: we are regenerated by experiences, sometimes the most devastating and unpleasant ones.

After the press club speech, my position at the Endowment was even more tenuous. Ede Holiday called to tell me how disappointed the staff at the White House was because I had said those nasty things about Rich Bond, the chairman of the Republican party, whom I had called cowardly for suggesting that the president should abolish the Endowment. At least I hadn't returned from the press club to find my personal belongings on the sidewalk.

Staying until May 1 was staying too long. I wrote to the president to fix April 24 as my departure date. On my last day, I met with a group of Dartmouth students who were studying the issues of obscenity and censorship. We talked about the Endowment and I answered questions for an hour and a half. Their professor told me later that their debate about the issues we raised raged into the night — exactly the response he (and I) had hoped to get.

I packed my boxes alone and took them to my car. The antique desk I had brought from Oregon stayed with the Endowment. And apropos of all that had gone before, a fire drill sounded late in the afternoon. I walked down the stairs and out of the building. It was possible to get out after all.

Jack Neusner, the member of the National Council who had been first an ally and then a critic of mine, wrote after we first met, "My blessing for you is this: may you enjoy the last day as much as you did the first day, and may you go out as clean and beautiful as you have come in." I find this as ambiguous as my service was. Perhaps the only two days I did enjoy were my first and last ones, but I do not doubt the importance of the journey or the value in undertaking it. My last words on leaving town are those of the poet William Stafford:

> Sometime when the river is ice ask me
> mistakes I have made. Ask me whether
> what I have done is my life. Others
> have come in their slow way into
> my thought, and some have tried to help
> or to hurt; ask me what difference
> their strongest love or hate has made.
>
> I will listen to what you say.
> You and I can turn and look
> at the silent river and wait. We know
> the current is there, hidden; and there
> are comings and goings from miles away
> that hold the stillness exactly before us.
> What the river says, that is what I say.

AFTERWORD

*I*N THE 1950s the United States government began to construct a system of federal highways that would facilitate travel and commerce among the states. These highways led to improved state, county, and municipal roads, enhancing the speed and ease of travel throughout the country. By analogy, the National Endowment for the Arts, created in the 1960s, has provided the federal arteries to support arts projects, which have been supplemented and enhanced by state and local artistic efforts. Just as the federal, state, and local highway systems have slightly different but interrelated functions, so too the federal, state, and local arts agencies produce a mutually nurturing ecology of arts support, which is one of the great creations of the second half of the twentieth century.

The arts network has increased the quality of life for all American citizens and needs continuing support and maintenance, just like our highways. But the cultural terrorists will certainly show up again for the 1993 reauthorization of the Endowment, finding offense without provocation and seeking to eliminate or emasculate the NEA with content restrictions. They will argue that we can't afford the sixty-eight cents per person that we spend to acknowledge and define our humanity. They will fulminate against a few artists' work, about which, if cross-examined, they will reveal an embarrassing ignorance.

The only issue worth debating, however, is whether the Endowment should exist at all, because if the answer to that question is yes (as it surely is), then it must exist free from content restrictions and subject only to vigorous procedures for seeking artistic excellence. The "decency language" that currently exists has already been declared unconstitutional by at least one court. Its primary failing is that it seeks to protect the listener. The First Amendment protects the right of the speaker, especially the occasional one who espouses unpopular ideas. We are strong enough, as a country, to live with diversity of opinion. Moreover, the suggestion by some that the Endowment is the sponsor of artists' ideas is clearly fallacious. The Endowment is the enabler; the ideas belong to the artists.

Here is how the Endowment can be enhanced in the next reauthorization, to do its marvelous work better. First, give it enough money. It needs $350 million annually, about twice its present budget, to stabilize large institutions, promote education, support the arts groups and individuals with which the United States is so richly blessed, and enhance international cultural exchange.

Second, remove the National Council on the Arts from the grant-giving process. When the Endowment received one thousand grant applications a year, it made sense for the National Council to review them. Now, with more than eighteen thousand grants per year, it is a charade at best, one that is disruptive and time-consuming and deflects the council from the area in which it could make a real contribution, namely, thinking systematically about how the arts can best be nurtured in the United States.

Third, pass into law Senator Christopher Dodd's idea of having an actual endowment, funded by extending copyright protection from fifty to seventy years and putting proceeds from the additional twenty years into a permanent fund for the arts. Economic research (which is available at the Endowment) shows that if the rights to twenty more years of copyright revenues were auctioned (so the Endowment would not have to police the collection of royalties), the initial return would be only $4 to $5 million per year, but over the next fifty years the return would be substantial, and the income from this endowment fund would enhance the annually appropriated budget of the NEA. This is a way in which the arts would help to pay for the arts.

Fourth, don't use the Endowment's funds as a pork barrel. This started in 1990 with the Coleman-Gunderson amendment, which increased the percentage of the Endowment's budget that goes to the states. Senator Helms seized on it in his dismembering amendment in 1991, which would have sent 70 percent of the funds to the states. While giving more money to the states is tempting, it is counterproductive. It reduces state expenditures, hinders the Endowment's ability to lead the country with national programs in folk arts, literature, media, and dozens of other areas, and ultimately makes art more rather than less susceptible to political interference. A state funding portion of about 30 percent makes sense, particularly if the Endowment's budget is $350 million.

Finally, authorize hearings on American cultural policy. The debate over the past four years has been about what some people abhor. It's time for us to think as a nation about what it is we really value. Can (or should) a society as diverse as ours come to some definition of American culture? Is our country's contribution to culture one of process rather than objects? Has democracy, and particularly the protection of speech, religion, and assembly under the First Amendment, had a defining effect on American culture? Does the Fifth Amendment's protection of private property always supersede the moral claim to an object of a tribe, community, or nation? Who can speak for cultural policy and teach it? Can only those who are genetically related to a culture sing its songs, dance its dances, and tell its stories, or, in a living culture, can all people use and manipulate the symbols? If culture is defined more broadly than just objects and architecture, then what are the limits?

This kind of inquiry wouldn't necessarily lead to answers, much less to legislation. But it might produce some badly needed insight into our national character and goals. It is possible that by listening to, understanding, and participating in the arts, we can revitalize the American dream for the twenty-first century. That dream might include living in harmony with nature and pursuing profound and useful knowledge as goals in both art and business. Rather than defining success purely in terms of money, or education in terms of a job, we might gain such satisfactions as human fulfillment, human expression, human generosity, and a full life.

INDEX

DATE DUE

DEMCO 38-296